Slow Dancing With Silence

I0080611

Slow Dancing With Silence

By Tracey L. Pagana

Copyright © *2022* Tracey L. Pagana
All rights reserved.
ISBN -978-0-578-37170-2

1

Dedication

To all the light workers who support each other in the many capacities of unconditional love. Without the team that combines our working efforts to unite source we would not be capable of completing our loving mission of educational wisdom. The constant flow of loving living energy surrounding unconditional love. I am grateful for my team I am in awe and gratitude for the cause and effects that seems to multiply in strength our team works together in. May you all find this love and light to feed and guide you.

Thank You

I thank every person who continues to grow with me on this journey for always being at the right place at the right time to manifest the magic of getting this work into the world. Thank you Laurie Smydo for the amazing cover art and all the fabulous contributions you made to get this book complete. Thank you Wendy Trumbley and Maria Webb for contributing your unique gifts to this work.

Thank you to my wonderful partner Joe who steps aside and lets me write this message for source so we can all grow independently while supporting each other. Thank you Divine Source for continuing to teach us how to grow and evolve the world into Divine light.

Foreword

My name is Wendy Trumbley and I have known Tracey for several years. We live in the same small town and worked at the same company, for over a decade together. Many of those years were spent knowing her from a distance. I wasn't aware of her spiritual side for some time, just that there was always a bright, warm, and welcoming smile upon seeing her. Through my own journey we have grown closer, and I can say with absolute certainty that she has been a huge help in guiding me forward.

I have always loved reading and writing and have considered looking for casual work as a proofreader. With a love for the written word, but not any formal educational certificates on the subject, the next best thing for a resume is experience. As an independent author, I immediately thought of Tracey and wondered if one day she would write another book. Several months later, during one of her online lives, Tracey mentioned she had the idea for a fourth book but hadn't started writing it yet. I took that as my cue to contact her. After about a week of "Should I? or shouldn't I?" thoughts, and making peace with whatever her answer would be, I sent her a carefully worded text asking her for the opportunity to proofread her next book. It was a giant leap of faith for me. After all, this was her fourth book, and she has had people in place to care take her previous messages from Spirit. I wasn't sure I was completely qualified to work with her words either, as I am still navigating and understanding my way through a more spiritual way of life. What if I didn't understand the messages and wisdom she was imparting? What if I made a mistake proofreading? Regardless of all the possible "What ifs", it was something I felt compelled to take on. It is quite possible you will find errors in my work as well, and that's okay. I feel very fortunate that Tracey has trusted me with this task and cleared the path to expand my horizons.

When Tracey asked me to write the foreword for her book, I was initially extremely intimidated at the idea. I only had the working title, **_Slow Dancing with Silence_**, and wasn't quite certain what that meant at the time. Never mind the fact that, for the first time in my life, my words would be published for public consumption. I have read all of Tracey's books and enjoyed each of them. Her third book, **_Coming Out of Darkness_**, really hit home. Just prior to reading her book, and as someone who has been researching and discovering what it means to be spiritual, I had begun to identify the darkness in myself. It was reassuring to read her words and begin to better understand what it meant to feel the way I was and learn how to bring the light to me instead. I am currently at a point in my life where I can appreciate and begin to understand why things have happened to me the way they have. I am certainly not an authority on the subject, but I do know what I need to do, to be the best version of myself that I can be in this life.

My journey into the spiritual side of life started quite naturally. I've always had a curiosity about the "unexplained". Conversations regarding people's beliefs as to whether heaven exists, if ghosts/spirits are real, and of people having the ability to communicate with "the other side" have always fascinated me. I grew up in the Anglican Church and have always believed in God. I was, and still am, certain that Heaven does exist. I had only ever watched programs about people, who I believe, are gifted with psychic/mediumship abilities, or heard friends tell of their experiences; nothing firsthand. This left me skeptically optimistic in my beliefs. Personally, my life took a turn I did not expect, and I believe that event was the catalyst for my seeking the answer of "why". To see if this, along with all my other questions, could be explained through spiritual avenues. I started seeing various mediums/psychics who were recommended by friends, to prove to myself that there are people on this planet who can tell you things about you, that they have no business knowing; I bore witness to this on several occasions. Every person I have ever sat with has been highly accurate, and I believe were necessary stepping-stones in my expedition. After having been exposed to a variety of gifted people, I was able to discern who "my people" are. Aside from Tracey, through spiritual conversations, I have been led and drawn to three more individuals, who I now consider to be constants in my life. I will have sessions with them regularly to make sure I stay true to who I am and what I am here to do. They all provide similar themes in their messages, just different forms of communicating them.

It never dawned on me before that seeking answers through mediums would result in the necessity for deep, personal healing to occur. I've realized over time that it is required, to truly heal, and make room for my spirit to grow. Looking back now, it's easy to see that I was always trying to fill a void or tell myself I was ok. I do believe I did a decent job at covering my scars with those closest to me, but there would always be emotional setbacks. While I was managing to enjoy day to day life, I know that I wasn't fully present or connected; I was emotionally stuck in a rut. An unhealthy, mental loop of "What if's" would, at times, consume me. As much as I thought I had done the work to accept the past, I realize now I was just doing surface work, enough to keep me mentally afloat. In June of 2021 I had, what can only be described for me, a mini mental breakdown. I saw these words on the internet, and hope it's ok to be in print here, but this is the most accurate explanation for how I was feeling at the time.

"A spiritual awakening is not usually pleasant. Often it feels like confusion, frustration, anger, sadness, grief, or "being out of place". A spiritual awakening can be uncomfortable and challenging because it's an intense time of

personal growth. But despite how difficult it may feel, you're not going crazy; you're evolving."

This is where my season of slow dancing with silence began. Knowing I have PLENTY to be grateful and thankful for, I could not understand why I continued to experience the mental loops, because I thought I had made peace with the events of my past. One of "my people" suggested I needed a Reiki healing session and Tracey is who I turned to. The day of the appointment I was in a great mood, feeling happy, and really, quite oblivious to what was about to transpire. I'll be honest, I don't fully understand what or how Tracey does what she does, I just know it works. Even in the moment I wasn't convinced what we were doing was going to work. During our time together, she helped me release old wounds, and wounds I didn't know existed. To my surprise, I was brought to tears. I thought all the tears of my grief had been shed before. After the session, I felt instant relief; like a weight had been lifted. It's been over the last couple of months though that I've recognized the physical and mental shift within. I know with certainty that while I can continue to hold space for the events of my past, I have reached a level of acceptance where I am no longer plagued emotionally about it. A session with Tracey allowed me to mend, forgive, and accept all the broken pieces of me. In combination with the healing session, it has taken some time and conscious, continuous effort to practice gratitude; be mindful about daily interactions, and to change the way I think in certain situations. Trying to find the positive in everything, not giving power to insignificant or frustrating encounters and living in the moment have been immensely helpful in my transformation. I am not always successful and have a long way to go, but I have begun to experience the difference these alterations have had in my life. Once I change my behavior and attitude to specific, historical triggers, those instances become less frequent and bothersome in the moment.

For me, I knew it was time to make a change when I experienced a persistent nagging in my soul. There is no other way to describe it. I was tired of emotionally feeling the way I had and realized that the reasons causing the unhappiness could no longer continue thrive inside me. For my own health, the health of my marriage, and relationships with family and friends. In my situation, this was a major kick start to my spiritual growth. However, like most things, change will not happen unless the person is truly ready to make a change and is committed to the change. Having the proper support system in your life is important. I am fortunate to have a great husband, family, and group of girlfriends around me. Throughout our entire 16 years together my husband has been wonderful. There are moments, even now, I feel like I don't deserve him, because he treats me so well. At times it hasn't felt like it, but I know he always has my best interests at heart. Don't worry, I know he's lucky to have me too! There is unconditional love, trust, and stability in him. He knows me better than I know myself sometimes; a pill that, for those who know me well, is not always easy for me to swallow. I am getting better at accepting it though! I am extremely blessed to have him in my life. He has been a constant at times when I probably wasn't giving him reason to be. He was the closest to me and I placed blame on him at times; both consciously and unconsciously, as it was easier than looking inward and addressing the feelings and emotions I was having, that I didn't know how to articulate at the time. He loves me, and that's what love is. My healing journey has helped me become a better partner and lightened the load inside of me. I will spend the rest of my life showing up for him, as he has for me all these years, in the best version of me that I can be.

Why Tracey? Why is it necessary to slow dance with silence? Are you feeling stuck, or in a cycle, a continual mental loop? If you don't want to feel that way anymore, that is your signal to action.

Dig deep and try to identify or acknowledge what is keeping you stuck. Once you know what needs to be worked through, you can begin to accept and release it. Sometimes that is personal, independent work, and sometimes it requires assistance. That is where Tracey comes in. Trust me, you won't regret it. She has said before that slow dancing with silence hurts. It is painful and it is not easy. She is telling the truth. I absolutely believe there is a divine outline to everyone's life. It takes bravery and an open heart to take these steps, and every single person is capable, if they are willing.

Tracey, I thoroughly enjoyed the experience of proofreading while simultaneously absorbing all the messages in your words. Some chapters were good reminders for me, and others felt like you had written them specifically to, and for, me. You are a wise and beautiful soul, and I am grateful for you. You have an innate ability to make people feel safe and cared for in your presence; it is truly magical. Thank you for allowing me the opportunity to care take your words and messages from Spirit. Your trust, faith, and belief in me is truly a blessing.

Cue the music, your time to Slow Dance with Silence begins now.

Table of Contents

Slow Dancing with Silence

It's 3.13 am. I have been informed a few times that this hour in the middle of the night is known to many as the bewitching hour; the time when the veils between physical and spiritual worlds are very thin. Lots of unexplained noises, and bumps in the night, have been talked about during this time of the day. I was born at 3:15 am so, maybe that is why I am so supersonic sensitive to this time of the night. Just maybe, I am split between body and spirit in this awareness. I can see the bright green neon clock light on the kitchen stove reminding me I should be tucked in my warm sheets, dreaming about nothing and everything that seems to envelope me these days. Yet, I cannot seem to settle. Something is building in our world that has my energy developing an excited twitch about.

This whole thing started when I was in the shower, minding my own business, when I could hear that familiar spiritual tingle of divine presence joining my spirit. Then the tingle on the top of my crown, near my right ear, and then I heard the words "You are to write another book and it is to be called *Slow Dancing with Silence*!" My immediate and probably disrespectful response was a rolling of my eyes and a very loud "No, thank you!"

Source is pretty used to his child reacting this way and always gives me time to accept, settle in, and get out of my own way. This slow rain of water beating down on me that day left a heartache thud in the middle of my chest. Like all other human beings in the year 2021, it has been filled with a diverse set of challenges for me.

I decided, like all the books I have written, to wait for more signs, timing and the familiar pulling of my Father in Spirit to direct and advise me. The best way is through, of course, personal experience. And as always, like clockwork, Father Time anoints my fingers and they start to move as if by themselves instructed through Source. Through my pores, my eyes, the middle of my heart, and the bottom of my soul.

It's been three weeks since I attempted to start writing again on a subject matter that is not, as some might say, my forte! Silence for me is a sticky, prickly subject matter. Learning the language of silence over the past three decades, but more presently in the thick after birth of COVID-19, has left most of us a bit bruised, raw, and vulnerable. I have had a few more ouches (I call them in my awareness) than ever before. Yet, like a moth drawn to the flame I seek silence out, even in the darkest corners of my life.

Why? Good question. I will attempt to write about my choices and lessons, incorporating new intimate dance steps. I have paid attention, allowing, and trusting the pattern. The new and uncharted territory does not match the old interior and exterior of my old life. It's in the dying, releasing, and shedding of my old skin; on layers deeper than I even registered. I have come to know, when you raise your vibration, the life after death places you in a higher frequency; incorporating dimensions in a personal experience and connecting to Source in a way I could never have imagined before.

Heather in Turkey

Heather, how do I describe her? She is wise, and battered, but the wisdom she possesses has given her grace and acceptance. She has spent more time fighting literal dark energy, certain forms of entities and has empowered herself with that knowledge. These energetic beings have literally taken pieces of her over the years but never won the war. She is beautiful, kind, wise and innocently ancient, giving her a soft glow but fiercely powerful awareness.

Heather is gifted, like so many of us working for Source. Slaying dark energy, conquering, and returning home to the light on a twenty-four-hour clock. As we know, Spirit never works on linear time schedules. I have known Heather for over 20 years. In that time, I have watched and witnessed her power transform and ignite. She calls me her sister and often says I am "her tribe". I just know, and have always known, she was special and gifted and challenged with the gifts; ones she naturally inherited. I will not divulge her personal life path or family history. Let's just say Heather has witnessed all forms of energy and its' power. That information is her story and hers alone to tell.

Heather has given me permission to tell the world of our experience together and her gifts. She is a reader of hearts and energy; that is my take on her intuitive gifts. She has vision when connecting to energy. At times she moves into a trance-like state, to allow her human vessel permission to transmit her messages for those seeking answers.

Heather and I met when we used to work together. She worked in the warehouse and I was in the office. I wanted to learn how to Belly Dance, which Heather teaches and is incredible at. She held a couple of classes after work and a group of ten of us started to

14

dance with her. It was so fun! I was not a natural, seriously, not kidding. Heather was patient though and kept on helping us get used to the rhythm and flow of the movements. As the weeks wore on, I found out that Heather was also quite adept at card reading. I must confess, I had only been to one person who did this type of thing, and it was face to face. The only thing Heather required was my name and birthday. That started our relationship on a whole new level of respect and journey. Every few months I would ask for another session and she would never cease to blow me away with so much detail and intuition. Super accurate.

Around two years later Heather had the opportunity of a lifetime. She bravely quit her job, sold her home, gathered her belongings leaving the very small town of Watford, Ontario and went on a trek to discover her soul and life purpose. This led Heather to eventually land in Turkey. She has created her life there, singing and resonating to the sea. She finds work where she can. Developing rich, healing relationships with her tribe of strong, spiritually connected women and men, wherever the wind and the sea take her.

We connect by way of social media through our Instagram accounts, a godsend. Most times it has been through texting but the last while I felt I needed to leave her voice messages, which over time led us to seeing each other one on one virtually.

Our time together was an experience neither of us will ever forget. We talked about her redirecting her ability to see clients virtually versus handwritten readings. She discovered it's much more accurate and intimate when Source is present in the interaction, so she is going to change her work and allow Source to become directly involved in the interaction with the messages, to and for her client base.

We laughed, cried, sang, and shared our dreams deeply, the literal and spiritual ones. She had messages for me, and this was the gift she gave me yesterday. She said "Tracey, your gift today is not external, it is within. You're God-source consciousness, first point creation. Find your own frequency; that sound field that is connected to your original blueprint. Raw, primal, primordial field. Holographic projections of tenability". This was something I had never ever thought about, and here Heather was delivering me this message, channeling for me, from Source. Then she went on to teach me how to do this. Sharing with me how it feels when you Om your own voice, as it resonates internally, when you place your tongue on the roof of your mouth. Truly, it was life. Feeling a vibrational energy, my vibrational spiritual DNA for the first time, honing itself home.

Heather was specific, she stated "NO WORDS, just breathe and tone". I cannot even begin to tell you about the liberation in this. When I shared it with her with, my open heart and my voice coming out of my throat chakra out into the world, recording it and sending it to her, she said she could literally feel the vibration in the recording. What a gift to share, to and for the world. It's like holding space (I write a chapter about holding space later). This is the coolest thing. For years I have been singing, I even have had the opportunity of recording my voice and presenting the voice to a bigger audience. I have always struggled with the words and retaining them in a song. It's as if I open my mouth and I am in a trance, some other space in time. Here physically but somehow present in two separate places simultaneously, so to focus on words was always difficult for me to attain. This shows me why. I just get lost in the sound, the vibrational energy, and the force of the source of it. I just get to open my mouth and help heal and love the world in the silent space of no words. Actions of vibrational energy expanding and echoing around the planet, seas, lakes, ocean, forest and to the core of the earth.

The other point and I feel it's viable to support this experience, is that it's almost like the darker energy, the insecurity of the old world, of my growing up asking me to be quiet, considerate, and

16

not make noise or waves, knows this power can awaken and heal the world. I mean this deeply humming or singing, this vibration out of me was squashed down and silenced for many years by many people's thoughts, opinions, and power. People that were my peers, people I was encouraged to respect and abide by, be obedient and answer to, all had my power. So, my ability to be heard in this vibrational, life changing, mandate was never awakened within. I understand, bigger than ever today, why this resonates and shatters old energy that is shackled in a way we do not notice. The shackled energy uses our subliminal quiet obedience to feed the fear and lower frequency. This new sound breaks the shackles like glass and sets all prisoners, encapsulated by it, free.

As you have come to know me, my writing is half Tracey, half Spirit. Some of its free flowing from the experience, and the description the experience provides me. Some of it comes from Source giving it explanation. I wanted to write about this new tool, stored in my holding space, to be used in some part of my day, every day. From now until my last breath I will be using this gift to send out love, support, connection and healing vibrational energy. It's so important to share our wealth, to help feed the awakening that is happening in our precious lives and beautiful environment.

Heather, from the deepest part of my soul I am grateful for you. I love and honor you and your gifts, and I encourage you to get on that beautiful golden dragon and fly around the world, enlightening others with your brave beauty and astounding gifts

How Do We Learn to Feel Our Self Love In Silence?

This is something, at first, I felt uncomfortable with. It was, at first practice, pain filled. It was like my entire body was grieving the addiction of noise, stimulating drama and chaos. I remember my first kick at the can at sitting in silence for many hours of isolation, in my last job. There were times in that position that led me to this spiritual journey of isolation, so many times during my personal work. Now I know that it was my pre-school education on the subject. Nonetheless, it was not pleasant. I can remember how lonely, sad, and isolated I felt. I can still feel how that disconnect made me feel like I was alone on an island without the social connection of physical stimulation. It is kind of distracting to be honest when you only have you to keep yourself occupied. However, this commitment of accepting me did lead me to a deeper consciousness of knowing and listening to the core within my own self.

Acceptance of whole self-love for me happened in stages. The releasing and processing of acceptance is continual. This precious and personal slow dance with myself, accepting the awareness of it, has been a challenge most times; spanning over three decades of my life. Nothing beautiful that is sustainable happens for me quickly. It takes constant work and constant effort to forgive the unforgivable for me, and to let it go. Slowly marinating of my whole self entirely, like the best tasting stew in the world, it takes time to tenderize the entire package of ingredients.

Patina is not always pretty. In fact, almost everyone wants to wipe it off and see what's underneath it. However, it is extremely valuable. It has a purpose and acts as a coating of protection. What is it and what is its purpose? It adds value by protecting the core. Why do you think it is, that if you do not recognize the purpose of patina, the first thing you want do is wipe it off? For instance, if you happen to come across an artifact that could be several years in age, and you notice the surface may seem dirty or unkempt. The truth is patina is protecting the inside core. So, now imagine our bodies doing the same thing protecting the core of our precious soul within.

We are elements of aged wisdom. Unfortunately for most of us, we do not recognize this wisdom, for many years. For most of us it, isn't before we are over 30 years old when we start to look around us, and through us, that over time we have matured enough to even have an awareness of this patina. If we are lucky to possess enough awareness, we see it has taught us to slow down the ride and enjoy the view, knowing we have earned the protection of the patina that is keeping us safe in our awareness.

I talk a lot about the slow dance we have been discovering, in this forced silence of the world we've been living in, allowing a timeout period of reconnection. It seems to me, in my observation, there is so much difficulty for so many trying to find a way through the new uncharted territory of unscheduled routine. So many new changes, new methods of acceptance, new rules, and people being told "no", when they are used to so much freedom. It leaves so many people lost in a place of uncertainty and anger.

How does slowing down help in this experience? Slowing down and taking the time to just be present in the elements and the experience itself presents us, allows us to experience and accept the uncommittable conditions of the experience we have no control over. We cannot commit to what has not happened yet. To further this thought, we waste precious time trying to find ways to control the outcome of this uncomfortable experience, instead of by working through it.

19

Imagine a world that could speak without words, just actions. Allow yourself to imagine a world of vision and deep intuitive connection. Envision that all accounts of your life can be seen, felt, and understood from the internal part of you that has been silent most of your life. Imagine the soul essence of you having a chance to express his/her wisdom from an aged patina source of living, that has traveled with you from lifetime to lifetime, enjoying the experiences you have taken each other on. Imagine what the voice might sound like, how that kindness would curl your lips into an instant smile of recognition and satisfaction. Imagine the dreams you could share together in this new slow dance of one source, combined with all your years of wonder, and educated times well spent in the learning process in the lives you have shared.

How do we get to a place in all of this where we just put down the fear that keeps us from the feeling, we all deserve? To feel in the silence that can cripple us with so many extensions of our body's equipment. Anger, lust, greed, unhealthy selfishness, anxiety, suppression, and depression.

What works for me is breath work. Varied degrees of deep breathing and releasing allows my core to recalibrate. Always starting with some sort of forgiveness in what is happening to bring these darker emotions in and clouding over my happiness. Breathing sets, me up to release all the things, loops, particles; that I personally have no control over. It allows me to start back at zero by letting go of whatever is getting in the way of peace and free flow clarity.

Try it out on yourself. Don't make the first few times something unattainable for you or you will become even more anxious. Start with a slow ride on an inner tube down a lazy river. Start with something easy like just sitting in a chair with your feet flat on the ground. Feel the floor, grass, dirt, or water. Allow the feeling to penetrate your whole self, adapting to the temperature of your environment. And just soak up the energy, allowing the energy to envelope you with goodness. Allow yourself to feel calmly present for yourself. Allow your lungs to relax and take a beautiful deep breath. Hold the breath, not uncomfortably long, but long enough to recognize what you might feel as comfortable releasing. The releasing for me is varied. It may be something heavy that I have no need to hold on to any more or something painful I have been working on accepting in my life. What also works best for me, in this releasing, is to visualize a source of love. It can be different every time or the same visual. For me it's usually a being of immense vibrational love that shines and shimmers, holding its arms open for me to walk into, and breathe whatever is keeping me conflicted or stuck; I let it go and it is received. I think the importance for me is, I have taught myself lessons most times (good or bad), in my experience of containing things. It may very well be, so I don't repeat it, or I do it again. I think that may be why, over all the years, I have held on to things longer than necessary. This process of releasing has taught me that it clears out the clutter in my body, allowing new real estate to enter the unchartered territory I have yet to experience. The importance for me to release to my Protector and Source is that I know my releasing will be cherished and protected in a way that I feel safe to release it. This practice allows me to live in a place of less congestion and peace-filled living. I have more room within to feel all the new space and I get to choose how to fill it.

Selfish Selflessness

When it comes to understanding the ingredients required to live a life with the fine balance of being selfish, as well as learning how to dance with yourself in a state of selflessness, it has taken me many years to find the formula that works best for me.

In my opinion, the word selfish is overused and undervalued in the same breath. How many times have you heard from a parent, caregiver, lover, friend that you may be doing or acting in a way that may be selfish or self-fulling? I wager you have had many people use the phrases "stop being so selfish" or "you are just so selfish". This is so interesting to me as I have, at times, taken this to be very personal and very hurtful when directed or pointed out towards a certain behavior or action that has offended another. To be honest, it can be very painful to be accused of something that you may not even be aware of that creates another's discomfort or pain.

For me, it's a deeper opportunity to take that pain and dissect the truth and take accountability for it. I see it as an opportunity to be accountable for my actions, thoughts, words, or lack of actions that have hurt or affected another person. Sometimes, in the awareness, I discover that the attack on me was not about me but about the person who felt the need to attack me. Something within that person is hurting. In that hurt there is a deep need to find a way to bring me along in the stress, burden, or hurt they are going through. This has been a commitment for me to find a deeper sense of self control. Especially if the person attacking me is relentless and mean. These are always triggers for me. In these moments I have the instinct of survival, I want to fight back and protect my values, my body, my core, my world. Sometimes I can rise above this, but most times I succumb to the need to protect myself from the hurt, while still trying to understand, by striking back at the person, sometimes in the cruelest ways.

What is the difference between being selfish and selfless? My view is being selfish means that it is your way, and the only way, to experience any aspect of life. Your thoughts, words, and actions are the only way to be, or see life, and the living around you. You are the way, the truth, the light, for yourself and anyone you love. You don't listen with your heart; you listen with your ego. Your ego dominates you entirely and you have no room for anyone else, including the deep quiet wisdom of your internal and eternal soul. There is no other room for anything but the way you see, feel, and think unless it benefits you in every way. This is what selfish means to me. How am I able to say this? You might think I have been in this position in my life many times throughout this life. I have, at times, only thought about me and my immediate survival, several times in this body. I know this emotion well. I have worn it with many scenarios and many hats, in places of comfort and discomfort. This has taught me to respect a selfish state of mind and being, in a whole new way of acceptance. I no longer choose to live in this self-absorbed state of being. I choose to be selfish, in the healthiest ways possible. Practicing a balanced state of "healthy-selfish", I can maintain my equilibrium of whole healthy self-love. By being conscious in the moment and understanding the power of the energy of that awareness, it allows oneself to be aware of a much grander picture of selflessness. When you can surmise the amount of selfishness it takes for someone to act in a hurtful manner, directed at but unrelated to you, you can then be a constant flow of unconditional acceptance of that person and their self. This wisdom allows you a deep acceptance, maybe even love, of the worst-case scenarios into your life. In this practice, you create a constant endless flow of forgiveness, on all levels of living.

Choosing to Fall In Love with a Narcissist

What is a narcissist? Basically a person with narcissistic personality disorder, a type of personality disorder causing a mental condition in which people have an inflated sense of their own importance, and a deep need for excessive attention and admiration. This can and does cause trouble in relationships if it continues, without help or deep self-reflection. This can also lead to a lack of empathy for others.

I wanted to, as gently as possible, discuss my experience around this subject matter. With as much respect as possible, talk about something I feel deeply in the core of me, that we all need to address and be responsible for in ourselves, also in the love we have for others. There has been a lot of talk, theories, and discussions on this word. The actions this word can teach us, for me, is way beyond the experience of it.

I believe, with all my heart and soul, it is important to understand this world and the effects it can have. It is something one must deeply come to terms with understanding, because to know something so well we must be, or have experienced, what we know. In other words, I honestly believe to understand narcissism, and be the victim of it's' burdens, one must (in some ways) also be a narcissist. This sentence may cause an instant reaction of feeling a flood of emotional responses; anger, frustration, doubt, anxiety, memories, and even feeling ill in the core of your solar plexus. But believe me, I only write from my very own research and experiences.

When I suggest we are all a little narcissistic it's not, by any means, a judgment. It is just a place of truth and experience that I draw this information from. Living with narcissism in our society is widely accepted and is even in some cultures expected and honored, as a show of action and strength as well as dominance.

For me, because I work with the aftermath damage of years of dominance and internal bleeding caused by this word, in many sessions of suppression and depression, I have experienced what triggers and what releases in the awareness of the damage internally and externally. This word, and the meaning of it, causes so many to seek a healthy way out of this negative cycle of energy.

Living in all this awareness has had me take a very deep dive into my own destructive choices, with the mini tornado of narcissism attached to all the destruction my path and choices led me to. In all this reflection, I started to remember the times my back was up against a wall and the mean, intended actions and pain I purposely caused others. I remember feeling zero positive emotions around others' pain and misfortune. It was almost a joy, in a way, to see those who had hurt/mistreated me, those I was jealous of because of attention they were receiving, or those who I saw as loved and popular, now experiencing their own turmoil. I can think of a few times as a small child being happy that my sister, the one my parents favored, being mistreated or punished. These feelings were real and almost dangerously leaning towards a deeper narcissistic pattern of behavior, in a very unhealthy way. Gives me full body shivers of shame when I think of some of the ways I did not care or even want to entertain anything but lower frequency energy, suggesting this behavior was not only warranted but completely acceptable.

Narcissism is real, it's powerful, and it dominates when it is allowed the power it seeks to confirm the righteousness of this emotion. It can rule countries into a place where there is no room for peace, or communication. Dictators over centuries have proven this emotion time and time again that it rules, and it has cause and effects on others. Yet it is an emotional tool that everyone can tame and come to understand on a level of truth and companionship. This may sound out of context to write something as bold as this statement, but I genuinely believe we can retrain this beast that resides.

Loving a narcissist is accomplished by loving the narcissist in you. Addressing all those terrible thoughts, actions, patterns of nasty and mean behavior, thinking your way is the only way, your truth should be everyone's truth and singlemindedness are avenues to a self-destructive way of living. When you take time to listen with your heart, instead of the loud thoughts directing your mind, you can hear differently. It is so crucial to listen differently; others will teach you if you can remain humble, open, and pliable.

Again, I cannot begin to emphasize enough the importance of finding a way out of this darkness and black hole of heartless reasoning. You first must be able to admit to yourself you have the mirror in you that reflects the narcissism you feel and understand in others. It takes a brave and strong person to admit defeat and dependence on this harsh way of living life. Once you can accept and admit this part of yourself, you can begin to set examples by wielding power over these tendencies. That there is nothing to fear in separating themselves from their own narcissistic entity. It takes a brave man or woman to address their darkness and shed light on the fear that dominates such a harsh reaction of pain and vulnerability within. I believe addressing the core of this in my own being has humbled and crumbled the hard core around my heart, and old scar tissues of the choices I made, when I gave in to my own narcissism. It has softened me. Allowed me to bend like a willow in a bad storm, when being showered by narcissistic behavior. Sometimes it's present in the most important people in my immediate circle.

Loving yourself, accepting the truth, no matter how ugly and dirty it gets, will allow you the grace, the lessons, the education, to not only dissipate and erase, but will save you from further aggressive behavioral patterns as the facilitator, director, and receiver of narcissistic energy. How to love a narcissist starts with you accepting and honoring this very ugly essence in your own true self. It allows you to understand the reasoning and the fear that drives this emotion. It also allows you to give thanks to the lesson, allowing you to choose to repeat it often, or allow it less room in your vessel. Love yourself in all your broken lessons. Accept yourself as you are and release the excess, as you hold space in the silence that our life has become. This gentle grace of silence we have long forgotten and have been reminded of its' use in so many new forms. There are times I look at my beloved, who has a strong opinion on life and how life should be. I send him wave after wave of love as he struggles with finding his truth, teaching others the things that matter most to him. I have more compassion than ever before, as I can identify in his display of emotional turmoil and frustration, as well as my struggle in these moments, because of our combined need to be heard in the power struggle. I identify with not being heard or understood in my own life. Sometimes I just step back and say to myself with love, "oh honey, how hard it must be to live in the energy of your thoughts; how much this energy takes such a toll on your whole body". So, in those moments I intend. I am not always successful. I choose to not take the verbal expressions personally, the toxins that he so passionately spews out in his thoughts and words, but rather as a loving sign, in a strange way of caring. My newly trained mindset of habitual forgiving the unforgivable kicks in, during what I call these "attack lessons", slowly dissipating, releasing, filtering the darker energy that is yearning to be fed- and returning it to the light instead.

For the past two weeks I have been on a vacation with my sweetheart. We went to visit my parents, who live in Prince Edward Island, Canada. It has been an eye opener for me on many levels. I want to elaborate a bit more on this chapter as I have had a whole new education on the sickness of narcissism. I have stepped out and really listened and heard the language of two people who I absolutely adore, struggle with the mental and emotional crippling effects of narcissism. As I stated previously, I believe we all have a strand of this illness in our bodies as it winds its' way in and out of our lives, minds, thoughts. I also have had an opportunity to dig deeper into feeling the causes and effects, watching the interaction in these two relationships, and gathering facts has given me a newfound understanding. I cannot believe sometimes what comes out of the mouth of someone who is in full on verbal assault mode or having an emotional outburst. To watch a person I love hurling the most incredible toxic storm of the harshest, meanest words you could ever conceive. These accusations, insults and low grade energy hurling at you, like a ninety mile an hour major league pitcher's curve ball, leaving you so busy dodging the pitch you cannot help taking it all personally. In saying this I did just that, initially. But, in mid accusation, I stopped taking it personally. While witnessing this behavior, in the moment, I was able to realize the person throwing the pitch was so damaged that in the outburst, he did not even know what he was saying. This is the magic part, he did not even know what he was even suggesting, calling out, or insulting; he did not retain one single syllable. It is like the awareness part of his actual brain blew a fuse or short-circuited. Truly, he did not remember one mean thing he even said. Here is the thing, I heard it all and I always do. The truth is I need to release it all at the same time he is throwing the curve ball. Not hold on to one single word that is being said.

This is like a coming home to truth in the moment, to recognize the pain that you experience while you are amid the attack, that the recipient is someone who cannot understand how it feels to be the receiver of this kind of hardness. To witness narcissistic personality disorder is to witness someone who does not have the capacity to fully feel love. This person considers the emotion of love a weakness, a weak link in humanity, a flaw.

An example of this would be, when I react emotionally, it reminds the narcissist of how unemotional they are. Which, in my observation, can grate on the nerves of a narcissist and annoy them. When we can teach a narcissist to honor their pain, it's like honoring their own damaged soul. The part of them they don't understand or pain they cannot feel. I really have come to understand that a narcissist is so uncomfortable with a heart felt pain they feel in another, if they cannot control or fix that, it becomes a source of aggravation and all they want to do then is debate or state the reason they believe their actions are the superior ones. They feed off adoration, but they don't know how to feel if they are not adored or in a state of adoration. It's about what they can control not what they cannot. Forgiveness is the only way to save yourself and rise above in this toxic environment. It is also the only way to love the broken narcissist. You cannot tamper or lower the level of love to reduce the pain in this kind of interaction. Pain and love dance together; it would be incredibly sad if we did not feel the pain or at least try to understand this level of communication. The five-foot-tall level of pain can at times feel twenty feet tall because the two do not like to feel each other. If we did not feel the pain, we would truly not be opening our heart and soul the core of our existence to unconditional love, combining the biggest secret ingredient in the solution, total forgiveness.

My father a very interesting man. He has taught me a lot of things, some good and bad. Ever since I could remember he has always been inquisitive, on a level of almost bordering the likes of a mad scientist. His level of empathy has been twisted, even as a young child he had the deepest desire to know things with a strange, even aggressive intensity, a thirst of knowledge and for things that have not been found out, sourced out, or yet discovered. Really listening to him without being wounded or feeling like I had to protect myself from pain, this past visit has taught me to understand why he would have done things that absolutely crushed another person. He just thinks in a way that is off the beaten track of what most people deem normal. I don't think his mind was capable of being any other way. I understand now that he thought the things he did and the choices he made were all about teaching what he thought needed to be taught. In some ways this new insight frees me even more from the places I remained for so long, entrapped in my own life and lessons he chose to direct me and others I love in. I have been able to let go and move on with a few more tools to help others still stuck in the loop of the educational system I was raised in.

I trust that this chapter may hit a few sore spots, maybe even splitter some fragility, depending on how harsh the narcissism has been in your own personal experiences. I do believe the only way to be free from this way of living, and living with and around this dark energy, is to first be accountable of your very own narcissistic traits. Recognizing the changes of acceptance and deep internal forgiveness first in and for yourself and then for the darkness of others. This will set you free. Educating yourself and in turn teaching you to tame the beast within you and the beasts around you. Choosing to love the best parts of a person that are buried in their muddied pain-encrusted ways of living can be a challenge and sacrifice. The virtue patience comes to mind as you choose patience in every psychotic interaction the narcissist feels impelled to reel at you. It's extremely pain-filled, and it is always a challenge to rise above the personal insults and attacks. The good news is, they are often short-lived, giving you both a chance to recover. Recovery is important. Stepping away and recalibrating internally as you release what was not yours in the first place. There will be moments of growth and awareness as you come to gain the knowledge that you will need to forgive and release all the old toxins that linger around your bruised heart. Learn to lean on yourself, deeper than you ever knew possible. Hear the soul in you that surrounds you in the love you are not receiving from the person who you thought would not, could not, ever treat you with such disrespect. Know that this person is showing you a glimpse of their pain and trusts you enough to share this beast within. Please know this reflects the inner brokenness inside of them. Know deeply you are not the one holding this beast, you're the person the beast feels safe enough to share itself with. This is not meant to justify the behavior, but to explain that this person cares enough about you to show you all the pieces of themselves. Use your heart as a filter and allow the toxin to flow right through you into the arms of your divine love source. This source is equipped to care for all of us. Trust me when I say, many times, I surrender this pain to a higher power to hold for me. I know deeply I am always loved and cared for by this source.

I Release Myself from the Versions of Me I Created Just To Survive

Its 2:22 in the afternoon July 22. All these numbers must of course mean something. So, I Google "what does 22222 mean spiritually", as anyone knows, with Google at your fingertips you can find the meaning of just about anything you're searching for! This is what 22222 means according to Google. "22222 spiritually symbolizes a **duality.** This means you are likely to feel that there are two sides to your personality. Accordingly, your guardian angels encourage you to find a way to reconcile with your inner self, ideally, this is the best way you will achieve the harmony you're looking for".

Interesting (as my friend Cathy often says). I find this interesting because I just finished a live weekly Facebook video, that I host on my Facebook page, and the title and format of the live was the same title of this chapter. Let me back up to 12:59 pm today, maybe even before that, around 10:00 am. I started my day after my first early morning regularly scheduled virtual session, and it was much like any other day. I seemed to feel a bit hurried and scattered and my flow of routine was a bit off-center. I paid little or no mind to it and carried on doing several errands, ticking things off the list. As I was getting ready to prepare myself (routine for my Thursday Namaste) and I was, in all honesty, feeling a bit unprepared for what is always 30 minutes of intense time, speaking truth from a pre-posted subject matter.

Laurie has become famous for, and instrumental to, creating the platform I talk from, on these live video Thursdays, that have been going on for almost two years now, every Thursday. What started out as a fifteen-minute short appearance on my Facebook Innerspace work page, of some accumulated thoughts, has morphed into various subject matter that is pre-posted, shared with people and forwarded to others. It's always just me speaking about my experience and my gathered knowledge on the specific subject for that live session, but I do share some personal thoughts and add those in the mix. I felt it necessary to type out some of the context, as well as the thought process, and sharing in the talk today and attempt to capture some of the sage magic that was discussed in the video.

Often, we make choices in life to help us get through difficult times. They might be choices completely out of character. It could be the way we speak to someone when we have lost our patience, or negative thoughts, stepping out on relationships, abusing food, drugs, or alcohol. These are only a few examples. So let us just take a moment and talk about this. When we feel pressured, not enough, misunderstood, unloved, bruised, abused, dejected or like we don't matter, we can choose one or even more of the choices I just acknowledged in the first part of this paragraph. When we feel abandoned or not heard we sometimes turn to other quick fixes. Instant gratification helps us hide, avoid, and not address the situation and it also allows us a distraction from the pain. Stepping out allows a whole new energy and distraction to start something new and fresh without addressing the old wound and releasing the toxins in it. Overeating and indulging in food as a substitute and pacifier for your deep wounds is a choice. I choose food over my feelings for so many years that it turned in to an eating disorder that had total control. For me this was my life saver; my choice of toxic bad choices that saved me from the empty heartache of a whole entire four decades of very bad choices. I have said this before, and I will say it again, every single human being I ever met has some form of addictive, habitual behaviors. It's a total distraction, a malfunction of internal shutting down and a free connection for the dark energy to seduce us and allow us to feed what it needs from our bodies, minds, and souls.

If we are ashamed of choices we have made in the past, we must be kind to ourselves and learn to forgive ourselves. We must find a way to totally forgive ourselves. We must realize that these choices were made to cope, learn lessons, and come out the other side better, for those choices we may have made in the past. All choices, even the ones that to this day haunt you in the middle of the night and you break out in sweats of silent pain and suffering, are the memory of the past and the suffering you either initiated or chose. You're reminded of that in these dark moments of past and truth. In the moments of this reality and self-respected honesty, the only weapon you have, that fights for your freedom, bringing new life to your brokenness and your wake of destruction, is forgiveness. Forgiving first yourself for the ignorance in the choices you made that hurt others, and then turning full on face on and forgiving the choices and ignorance in others.

To release myself from versions I created to survive difficult times, I choose every day to:

Set Boundaries

Boundaries teach us to co-create internal communication from an internal and external committed force of love and self-respect. First for ourselves to identify and re-discover a new way to communicate truth for ourselves, the world we interact with, and for the external world we are in constant vibrational interaction with. Boundaries teach us to speak, hear, and act in a way of less offensive authority and a deeper understanding of defending ourselves while respecting others. It dignifies space and clarity for others to feel heard and respected. When healthy boundaries are established, less fighting occurs. Boundaries are so very important to understand and comprehend, in the deepest way possible, to establish a coming together of minds, bodies, and soul. Most importantly, communication that does not have to be spoken to be heard.

Make Choices that are Healthy for Me

Healthy choices change your internal and external whole self, healing you in a way that is magical. I say this because I watch the manifestation of health explode around me daily. In my practice of watching the broken seeking healing, they manifest these healthy healing internal miracles and release all the old toxins that invade their sacred containers. They choose to release themselves from scars, triggers, memories, experiences, abuse, destruction, and patterns. This energy that has been trapped in their bodies is productive and feeding, yes, the lower frequency energy. This energy lives in the density of all this sludge that keeps us from growing into our power. Healthy choices teach us that the lighter energy, which flows effortlessly through our bodies, was born within us. Connecting us to the origin of where we came from, pure love. Healthy choices take longer to attain, comprehend, and are not something (unless you habitually work on this mind set) come easy to us. It seems easier to give into something that stimulates our emotional state with a quicker response to instant gratification. Heathy choices, once honed and repeated (for me), seem to have a longer lifespan of peace and comfort, than the alternative heaviness that unhealthy choices provide us in the lessons they leave.

Choose relationships that match your energy staying away from relationships that tend to drain your energy

Relationships all have a place of value, and all bring education to you in some way, shape, or form. Choosing relationships that have harmed you may very well show you the truth you needed to know about yourself in the reason you chose the relationship. Sometimes we mirror exactly what we need in another to grow into a deeper state of awareness. Sometimes we pick these relationships to honor or even dishonor ourselves. We learn from each and every one we meet, invite, partake and say yes to in different kinds of contracts with different kinds of interaction. When you grow to a place where you are in your total truth of your own actions, sometimes it gives us an opportunity to see the truth and the commitment you have made to others in your life. For me personally, I have learned the hard way that I promised more than I could ever hope to deliver in the relationships that have meant the most to me and those have not always panned out the way I had hoped they would have. I have loved deeply and lost people I adored. I have had some death in living friendships and family that I am still grieving and sorting out. Relationships teach me one huge thing; I am forever mindful of and completely grateful for. That is humility and a deep, unabashed understanding of true forgiveness.

Relationships that take too much from you and drain your energy may very well be soul suckers that work for the darker side of energy and are there to continue to use and abuse you. They drain nourishment from your very body, mind, and soul. Be mindful, strong and use your new tool of a healthy boundary. Put it into place and allow your truth to define new growth of what you will accept and what you will have to say a healthy "no" to. You are the ruler of your own paradise. You get to decide who and what you need in your life and your relationships.

Spend time on things that help achieve goals and desires

This can be fun, choose anything and everything you never thought you could ever do. Allow yourself to dream. Create vision boards and put every desire of your heart and soul out in the world and in the heavens. Shout it out loud and ask for all the desires that will teach you things you never dreamed possible.

Journal, write, smudge, co-create a vision with soul, ask for guidance from your spirit guides and angels

Ask for worldly signs that not another person living could know, to show you that your loved ones are not only hearing you but letting you know they have never left your side.

Know what you need
Know what you want
Go get it

Use your lessons of survival as stepping stones for a greater outcome in life. Remembering to give thanks to yourself for having the wisdom, knowledge, and courage to manifest making this happen; one stone, one step at a time. Have gratitude as an attitude. Every conscious moment of your day is an opportunity. Try stopping many times in your day and give thanks for all things allowing you to sustain your health, wealth, energy and prosperity. This will elevate you to the highest form of pure loving oxygen, clearing your way and your mind. The light will shine on you even on the cloudy days. This illumination, total body, mindset allows you to feel the freedom and internal essence of the light that shines from within you. Allowing it to flow in a glowing stream of energy that goes beyond anything external. We must know and trust this is who we are; in the depths of truth, we are light beings, shedding that light and sharing it in a way we are only beginning to fully comprehend.

Words Are Your Most Powerful Tool

There are beautiful reflections and revelations in times of slowing down and finding your tempo, as you slow dance with your internal silence. In saying this, I made a promise to myself a few weeks ago and found a way to detach from social media. Choosing to leave my phone on my nightstand for one day a week. I thought that Sundays would be my new day of unplugging from the demand and hunger I feel connected to. Sometimes in this disconnection I feel challenged in staying in the commitment to disconnect. I almost feel a sense of loss, a weird kind of grieving. Loneliness in not being connected to the energy that is looking for counsel, healing or help. This, in some ways, shocks me into the reality of truth. That energy, and the connection to it, can have so many causes and effects on our power and the power we are subliminally connected to. What followed in the days after my "day of disconnection" were deep, uncomfortable dreams that left me in night sweats; disturbing and reminding me that God was calling me out, to be aware of feeling and knowing on a deeper level. That I had to fill my own power pack to go back out in the broken world with fresh eyes and new strength. Also reminding me the power of words and how they can heal, dissipate, reject, suffocate, clear energy, and remain in the eye of any storm. Words will always be the most powerful tool in your toolbox.

Let me provide an example of what I mean about the power of words. Most days I wake up, get a cup of coffee, and make my sweetie his breakfast. You all know the comfort of routine. It's awesome when you can just get to the place that brings you peace. On the contrary, life at times can almost put a damper of darkness on any given moment. Like a cold wet blanket, the dark energy can seep into your happiness without warning. In can be in a conflict of miscommunication, or in a harsh exchange of words. By making a choice that offends someone, or just being in a head space that causes fear. When this energy seeps into my pours, my head, my heart, I stop and say directly to the energy "Thank you". I can tell the dark energy is confused and its' power is immediately defused, losing all momentum. I say "Thank you for coming into my life to show me what I absolutely do not want in my life. Thank you for reminding me who you are and what you represent. The piece of you that affects my energy is way too high. Please leave, you are not welcome in my life, or in the life of the people I love". This is the highest form of insult, in the highest degree, to this force that is starving for the light you are, that feeds its nucleus. Your words and truth weaken the walls of the thick darkness by shedding your light and compassion. I have come to understand that forgiveness is the darkness's greatest nemesis.

I am reminded of the power of words every single day, in all kinds of situations and interconnection. I am reminded that I chose to rise and attach myself to a universal energy that does not use words as often as I would like to hear them. This energy uses signs, actions and frequency that leaves a different vibrational awakening, to teach me to pay closer attention to the methods in which it is teaching me. This energy of love, awakening within me, has allowed me to meld the two words into a cohesive, subtle, and pliable commitment to work together. Using different communication skills, the knowledge of ego and working with soul are all combined and applied practices in how I choose to live out my life.

When words equate to value and that value is put into action, something changes in the molecules of energy to bring out the very best vibration in the frequency of what you are trying to teach others, in those who are searching for this kind of interconnection or direction. People are starving for clarity and peace. They are starting to understand that no matter what they say, if they do not understand the origin or power of the words they speak, their words have no real sustainable value and will not add to the deepening of the purpose of their being.

When I suggested words are your most powerful tool, I really meant it. I have come to understand words and their power, the delivery, the sting of their power. This creates an opportunity to keep a mental journal of what the lesson was for the person receiving, and the lesson was in the delivering. It works as well in honing your listening skills. We are gifted with two types of hearing. We hear physically and we hear spiritually. When you listen, and I mean really listen, you hear with a whole new way of understanding the actions others display. But again, to deepen your own awareness on how to love deeper about things you may not understand, agree to the invitation of the other person trying to find a way to communicate with you. This invitation may be to dance with them in their own grief or frustration as a silent dance partner, allowing that person to take the lead.

Listening to someone passionately tell their story is such an honor, a treasure, a gift, to the one receiving the messages. It means that another person is entrusting you with their deepest feelings, struggles, blockages or pain. It is also an opportunity to share another's deepest joys, accomplishments, golden thoughts of dreams yet to come, scars that have been festering or healing, and a need to release what is underneath the skin or buried in the scar tissue. Listening is a gift and when you listen, I mean really listen, you will always have an answer when the questions come, and they do come. You want your words to be healing and growth serum. For your words to leave a mark and then a path of direction inside their heart. This provides education and direction. This is what your higher power, your healer, your divinity knows to be truth; this is what a survivor knows is truth. Words are your most powerful tool, please be wise in the care of them. Please learn how to mix the verbiage in the language of the heart and soul so you can spread this love in a greater way! Be the leader you were born into, it's your birthright, your pledge, your spiritual code of ethics. WORDS ARE YOUR MOST POWERFUL TOOL! Turn your words into action; it will change the world.

Which brings me to the closing of this chapter. Actions are the combination of outcome with the follow through, the follow up and the closing, when you deliver your words. I am just learning the power of action. After I say something and then actually become the action behind my words. Action is a whole world of awakening for me. It has the likeness of ten-year-old cheese, that after bite that lingers on my tongue, tingling in the gooseflesh, that leaves its' mark on my body when I deliver something and then act on it, following through. I honestly had no idea how much more power my words have when I act upon what I just delivered. I have become more aware to the power of words when giving a sincere apology or taking the time to comment on how proud I am with a client or family member. Forgiving on an even deeper level than I ever thought I was capable of, when I am hurt deeply by someone I have loved or lost in love. Learning to detach personally on the actions or distractions or selfish motives of others. My action, my reaction, combined with this silent, new (yet still foreign), awareness is teaching me beyond any expectations I had to learn on this journey of continual enlightenment. Trust me, combining my words into living action (backing up my words) has been a very powerful experience and a deeper connection with Divine Source.

Take a Timeout for Your Whole Self

Are you, like so many of us, in the habit of waiting until you are unwell to carve out the time you need to rejuvenate, hydrate, and nourish your whole self? Do you ever take time to sit in silence and take a mental scan of your whole self? Is this scan revealing the need to recalibrate a few things internally as well as externally? In this light, is God source revealing signs physically, or spiritually for healing or corrections? Do you need to listen and take time out and consider your total health? Is it necessary to make room or create more peace in your daily routine, to quiet the chaos that often demands and commands attention? If we do not stop and listen to the signs and take note to the spiritual directions that are mapping out the truth, we can burn out and our bodies cannot catch up. Then causing a breakdown of depleted energy and the outcome is internal and external exhaustion.

Taking time to feel your body promotes commitment to detoxing, defining and realigning your complete whole self. Our ego mind thought does not comply with this kind of self-love. Our ego tends to be the only narrow-minded part of our existence, deeming any help to the other parts of our essence as unnecessary, leaving no room for compromise. This is a conversation of love in the silent reflections. You will come to find a way to converse the needs of your entire body, not just what your mind thinks, but as a conglomerate of whole essence. Seated at the table in the middle of your hearts' silence, you will be able to identify the much-needed slow healing process. A stepping out in truth takes time to listen and hear what your body needs, not the noise of the ego or the congestion around other energies, trying to monopolize your power pack.

This may seem like a harsh statement and although some people in your circle may very well have your best interest at heart, I can promise you most people have their own interests in place first. Leaving a trail of guilt as they, can and do, ask for dividends and pay backs often. Be wise to what you give, offer and ask others for; there will always be some sort of price tag attached. Be healthy enough to offer what is needed and what is fair, so you can keep that balance of healthy boundaries established within your own being.

We must train our brain into not feeling we need to justify, avoid, sacrifice, lie or make excuses on the path to find the peace and quiet we are seeking, to recover in our own daily lessons. Pay close attention that you're not confused about what self wants versus what self needs. Believe me when I suggest there is a difference between the two.

What self wants is to always feel loved. It wants to be coddled and loved, respected and understood. Self does not want to sacrifice energy to feel the effects of what self seems to need. The wants are varied, complicated and misunderstood. Self has the deepest internal and external desire to be heard, respected and admired. Self needs to be stroked constantly. It's the natural endorphin that feeds the starving ego that resides within you. Self wants are carnal, requiring vast amounts of energy, constantly trying to come up with more ways to sustain the thirst and desires. These ego-based tendencies reside with so many others being fed by the same source. We all want to be heard, to feel peace. We all want to make a difference, but we all do not want to release what must happen; to find the humility in the need we desire to achieve this goal.

What self needs is a silent pillow of God timeout, a place to define what the truth within you has led you to. A space where you can find a way to hear the deepest layers of your pain. Understanding it's not your responsibility to enlighten a parent or a

43

guardian who lets you know, one way or another, all the sacrifices they made to raise and support you. We owe respect and kindness (and of course love) to these beings who made huge personal sacrifices to raise and support us. We however, come to understand in the refection and need for a timeout, we give what we can and we offer what we can in the give and take these strings can sometimes bind us to. We come to understand the need for honesty, clarity and communication as we explain the reasons we cannot comply to their constant verbal, subtle forms of control and guilt they may be expelling, sometimes even subliminally. We owe these beings love respect, gratitude and a clean attitude when we express ourselves directly to them. Some things they may find they are feeling deep rejection and anger in. This is a hard pill to swallow when we know, for the deepest reason, people try to buy, console and sabotage or steal a piece of you that is not available for purchase. It takes a huge kind of wisdom to even identify the cause and then the effect of these toxic, emotionally bound relationships.

Sometimes the wants and the needs are too big to dissect. Unless you truly step out and step into the quilted quiet silence, dance with the energies to understand the need and the want, and the difference they support you in. In all this truth you will define the new boundaries in these important relationships that gave you life, by carrying your beautiful vessel, so you can also learn what you need to give and receive in the healthiest exchange of love, kindness, honesty, and truth. Sometimes, sadly, the relationship cannot be mended. Some people do not want to do the work it takes to separate from the dysfunction that is blocking their truth and choose to stay in the victimhood of this relationship, trying to make others validate them. Sometimes it is the karmic contract they set out to discover and recover from, to teach them what it is they needed to be taught. Sometimes, unfortunately, you outgrow relationships that you loved deeply and cherished. Sometimes relationships outgrow the lessons you needed to provide for them.

Pay attention, deeply, to the need and the want you're trying to focus on. Please do not make excuses or hide behind your truth, no matter how uncomfortable the outcome might very well be. It could be a very painful space where you seek closure, for some time. Being selfish, taking this time out for whole self can be messy and painful, but taking the time to address the issues and air out the truth will help your wounds and repeated patterns, paving a new way to heal. Find your truth, discover your potential. The pain in the silence we feel, will also heal. When you are feeling the energy, it is trying to remind you life is not easy. Address it, understand it and change it. Your entire life depends on it!

Slow Dancing With Your Inner Child

The truth is most adults do not take the time to slow dance with our inner child. Discovering puddles of rain to dance through or walking barefoot in the grass. Instead, we are so busy avoiding the puddle and the soft cool grass. As a result, we are side-stepping around the message right in front of us. Inner child work is something that does not come naturally as an adult. It can make you feel a tad uncomfortable and even vulnerable. Allowing a timeout, just to play, is not the world we live in. It's one that crunch's numbers and expects maturity and protocol. In a world driven by hard work, and a certain code of ethics, therefore excluding you from any fun that is deemed immature or not warranted. To bring inner childlike spontaneity into daily life, as something that is acceptable and without feelings of shame, is hard for an adult. Take the time to engage with your inner child and invite that child into the core of your heart every day until it become a consistent habit. Your inner child is dormant and is waiting for you to play, engage, ignite, and laugh with your spirit.

How do you even begin to recognize this inner child? What would it take for you to feel the bubbled-up laughter or even recognize the smile of satisfaction spreading across your lips that bring out that child in you? Practice. Practice getting to know the true desires buried deeply in your heart, the ones that soften it. Your heart that wants to sing with your soul. The heart wants to bring this child up and through your heart space. With your open arms, share your child with the sunrises and sunsets. Allow the wonder of a child to envelop you. The child in you will experience and feel, with new eyes and vision, as it stands in awe of this reawakening. Recognize this child within you, maybe for the first time as an adult. Choose to wrap this child in your arms and sit with you. Allow the depth of the love to saturate you!

Take the time you need to slow dance with this inner child, the one that has not had a chance to have expression. The one who has been in years of education; bound to expectation, honor, and responsibility. Sometimes we allow the timeout in a socially acceptable space, consciously or unconsciously. For example, a place that is stimulated with induced truth elixirs (like alcohol or other substances) that quiet the responsible adult, allowing your inner child a timeout to play. This can be fun and even entertaining, as most times we loosen our lips, tongues, and ties, and behave rather carefree and childlike. We know that, although this can be a lot of fun letting our hair down this way, in some cases, we can overindulge and then over or under react in a time when clarity and judgement might be on the back burner. Still, this is what we have been programmed to believe is acceptable, for the child in us to join the adult party around us.

We always get to choose. I truly love this about living, loving, learning, and discovering all the unchartered territory yet to be discovered. We get to choose all our actions, lessons, and adventures. All our decisions are based on joining forces with our internal and external connections.

Dance with your inner child! Get to know your child. Find what joy stimulates you, create space, laugh out loud, sing in the shower, and catch fireflies. Look for signs in the wind, the sun, the trees, and the forest. Build a tent and sleep under the stars. Count them until you fall asleep with angels on your pillow singing you a soft lullaby. Be one with your child and slowly, very slowly, teach your child how to dance. Take the time to hold your child in your arms and teach your child the intimacy of the dance and rhythm of your own unique soul.

This will bring you a peace you never dreamed or imagined. It will quiet your loud voices that are constantly stopping you from discovering your internal power. These voices what to squash your heart, dim your light and limit you from your world of manifesting all the private desires you keep buried in your solar plexus, your internal treasure chest. Choose you first. Go on a quest or a picnic with yourself and choose to dine and get to know you on all levels of yourself. You will thank your highest being for allowing you to discover this part of you that has been tucked away so long ago. Bring her/him out and find a way to recognize the things that bring you comfort, wonder, and complete and utter unfiltered joy. Choose to find this child that reminds you its ok to dance in the rain or make snow angels in the snow. It's ok to eat dessert before dinner, or hot fudge in the heat of summer, as it drips down the side of your face. Find this part of you that is not ashamed but inspired by your questions and wonder of the things you have yet to discover. Live larger than life. Have you ever witnessed children playing in a playground lost in their game and thoughts and just plainly concerned in the moment? These children feel safe, protected, self-absorbed in the healthiest way. We tend to lose this as we grow into bigger into the responsibility of living and taking care of life; the challenges that face us, the directions that claims us, and the duty that befalls us. This does not mean we need to tuck away the child within us, wanting to find a place of joy.

Loving yourself in all forms means to love every single piece of you. Accepting, allowing all these pieces to come together forming one whole being and one whole heart set. This means allowing the freedom of your inner child to play. Allowing a space for that child to observe, grow and bring love to the tired adult who struggles to find the time to breathe some days. In this acceptance, you will learn the new slow dance moves as they combine your adult and your child as one unit of smooth motion, bringing new lightness to the exhaustion of adulthood. Dance every single day with the child in you. Loosen up the grip you have on what you think living is all about and accept the spontaneous combustion that only a child can bring to your awareness. Love yourself like nobody else in the world knows how to do. In the end, you are all you have. So, you may as well get to know every single nook and cranny that occupies space in your amazing vessel. Be true to you. Love yourself like you mean business and laugh often at your own rigid grown up self. Laughter heals all wounds. Take the time necessary to fall in love with the inner child who has been waiting for you to gather it. Rekindle that love, solidify it, and befriend the best part of who you are. Children are fearless and have this awe-inspiring wonder about them. Trust me, you never want to lose the faith of your inner child.

Dance in the rain! You will never be sorry you took the best chance on you! You are worth everything!

Healing Balls of Love from Heaven

During the summer Joe and I were invited to join our good friends for a weekend getaway. To spend a couple of days in one of our favorite spots, Tobermory, Ontatrio. Joe and I decided to take our Victory motorcycle and go for a long ride, taking in all the sites along the way. It was a beautiful day, threatening some rain, but we started out on our adventure anyway. Joe has this kind of weathered internal compass when it comes to dodging rain clouds. It's kind of fun watching his years of experience beat the clouds and divert the worst weather. It probably comes from over 35 years as a seasoned rider. Growing up with my father, who is also a motorcycle enthusiast, I consider myself fortunate to have had many years of being on the back as a rider at a very early age. I have learned to totally be one with the driver, so it's rather effortless for me to trust the driver with my life. A rider must be one with the driver to keep the flow, and bend with and conform quickly to anything the driver might need to adapt to or avoid. It's a beautiful connection when you trust the person in charge with your safety and your life. Giving this trust develops an unspoken silent confidence and intimacy, as you explore the world, with the wind in your face. I often feel the stress of life fall off Joe's back as we ride for hours in this silence.

It just so happened that day, for the first time, we tried out our new headsets; purchased for the bike to listen to music and talk to each other. Joe was listening to his favorite songs, and I was listening to podcasts on mine. I started to listen to Super Soul on OWN. For those of you who don't know, it is the channel created by Oprah Winfrey. Oprah has this calming strong voice and I settled in to hear her thoughts and interview. I am, and have always been, an Oprah admirer. She has a power about her that just is. It's the kind of power that draws you in, sits you down, and opens you up to receive her presence. Not in a way that demands attention, rather in a way that educates you on every level. Her attention to detail, her interest and thirst in the truth, and her obvious love and deep respect for her interviewee's, leaves you wanting to be acquainted to her in a way that feeds your soul. I met her once years ago. I have a friend who, along with her sister, adores Oprah in the same respectful way I do. But for them it's an even deeper connection. They spent hours on the phone securing seats at her show in Chicago and I was lucky enough to go with them once to see her. At the show we attended, Barry Manilow was her guest. We loved it! My "Oprah moment" was an interaction that lasted all of six seconds. When I think about it as I type it now, I can still feel the way it felt. She shook my hand, but it was more of a firm "I am present" hold rather than a shake. She looked straight into my eyes, held her gaze, smiled (just a little) and I said, "God Bless you", she responded "You too". Oprah was present as I watched her move down the line of adoring fans. Present for every single hand she touched, every word, every look, she was present.

Back on the motorcycle, as I settled into my happy place on my warm heated seat, I was soothed by this voice. The world has the same response to a presence that allows us all to be present. She began her interview with a poet by the name of Mark Nepo. He is a best-selling author, poet, and philosopher who, in his battle with cancer, had a spiritual awakening. Mark had this same presence. A deep love and respect for God that left me with goosebumps during the thirty-minute interview (which I never wanted to end). He talked about life, love, peace, and grace. He answered Oprah's questions with paused dignity and gathered his thoughts before he answered her. His wisdom left little, tiny revelations, that rolled like soft velvet off his tongue, and trickled like honey on my heart.

My friend Dana always says, "You're like honey on my heart". Marc was like honey on my heart that day, like a re-opening, a planting of soft possibilities, and love notes, from Mark, from Source.

I loved the whole interview. It was food, hydration, and a completeness for my soul, in the perfect environment to receive the words being fed to me. I remember Oprah asking Mark a question like "what it is you do for the world Mark, what you would leave behind for others?" His answer came again after taking time to think it through. The way I remember it in my soul, he said he "likes to bring little bits of heaven down and spread them around to others, to the planet, to the living energy in all things". That struck me so hard that I had tears of joy and healing escaping me all at the same time, running down my helmet-clad face, exposing them to the wind that was rushing by. It was as if the wind itself was wiping them away with strands of angel's hair drying my checks. Since that moment, all I want to do is the same as Mark. I want to leave healing balms of God love in every nook and cranny I can find. In every interaction, every moment in a session, every conversation I want to look deeper, act on a higher form of consciousness and rain down healing balms from heaven. Bringing to this world, as Mark does, little pieces of heaven.

I must confess, at this point in writing this book, I have been addicted to getting my fingers on this keyboard and waiting to see what spirit and I (in conjunction) can pour out of me and into this manuscript. I was awakened tonight at 3:30am and could not get back to sleep, instead, being called to open my laptop. And here I sit, in the dark, at my kitchen table pouring it all out. It is now 4:28am, almost an hour into this, and it seems like three whole minutes have passed. The timing is perfect and the quiet in the air is the perfect space to write the things rolling around in my mind and thoughts. We leave tomorrow, for a nice break in routine, to visit my parents in PEI (Prince Edward Island). I have a long day ahead of me but was pulled out of bed to write, while the rest of my side of the world was probably still sleeping, to share spirit and love and thoughts with.

The warmth of Mark's love still lingers on my ears, soothing my soul. The humbling way he felt called to say he wanted to share pieces of heaven in this world in so much truth, conviction, and sincerity, touched the core of me. It awakened something inside me that had been dormant. It gave me a mission, a purpose; it called to me, as I call to you. Please consider your power is real and contagious and has the exact same ability. Please consider also sending pieces of heaven as well, as you think about this. Think about your being able to spread love to the home of your entity, and the entity and home for all other living energy.

Eighteen years ago, in September, I made a choice in my life allowing me to change direction and setting a new course of action. This was one of the most difficult choices I have ever made. It took a long time to consider all angles and deciding what was the best for all involved. Two weeks after this choice, I wound up at an all-women's retreat the other side of Bayfield, Ontario. In a huge field, several cabins with four occupants in each, a circle of reflection, a hall for presentation and one-on-one sessions with all walks of healers. There were at least one hundred women enrolled and many types of women gathered. Some local, some from quite a distance, for the two-day event. Some of these women offered services of healing, mystic readings, and shamanic journeying.

I was like a starving child being fed the whole entire smorgasbord of food and dessert, with unlimited helpings. I feasted, received, got drunk in the energy that saturated the whole entire sacred ground, in love-drenched spiritual energy. Not to mention the raining down of free-flowing hugs, understanding the intensions, words of wisdom, and getting to meet my spirit and animal guides in the deep shamanic exercise and journey I went on. I will never forget feeling the love, from the core of mother earth, meeting Lila (this massive wise ancient sea turtle). And no, it was not induced with any form of hallucinogenic substances. That was the best part. It was all natural, uninhibited, spiritual saturation.

I was sitting on a picnic table, reflecting on the second day of the retreat when a woman walked by me, talking to herself. Yes, she was having a full-on conversation with someone. I just watched her walk by me, she stopped talking, turned around, and walked up to me. She spoke to me directly which kind of startled me and said her angels had just spoken to her. She asked me if I would like to come to her home next weekend, Sunday afternoon to be specific, and that she had a very special gift to give me. Ok, you must keep in mind here that I did not often drive this distance by myself, and she lived two kilometers up the road. This is where it gets even crazier, I did not know her, had never met her, she was talking to herself, and she asked me to come to her home because she had a gift for me.

So, even more strange, my daughter had invited me to come to a big bash she was having at her farmhouse in Port Elgin. Yes, I had to drive directly past this women's house to go to the party on Saturday and same exact way home on Sunday. Knowing all this I said "Yes" to this woman at the retreat. Can you believe it? I said "yes" to this strange woman who just walked by me talking to herself.

The next weekend came, and my daughter's party was fun. It turned out that there was so much food left over she loaded me up with bags of it and said "Mom, please take this as we won't eat it and do something good with it. I know you will find a home for it and keep some for yourself".

On the way home, driving not one block out of my route, I turned into this beautiful property right on the lake. She had a jaw dropping view of Lake Huron with mature trees, lounge swing to sit on, which was quietly secluded and shaded near a private stairway leading down to the sandy beach. It was a million-dollar

54

view, but I noticed there was wear, tear, and a bit of tiredness around the garage. The lawn looked like it needed some attention, and the flower beds a desperate need of a thorough weeding. I pulled into her driveway, thinking to myself "What the heck am I even thinking. What am I doing in this stranger's driveway?" But I pressed on, got out of my car, walked up the sidewalk and rang her doorbell. I was greeted by the same lady who walked by me talking to herself the previous weekend at the healing retreat. She seemed to remember me (thank goodness) and proceeded to invited me in. She led me into her house, and we entered a great room where the main part of her living seemed to happen. The kitchen was attached to the living room. She led me outside to the beautiful cliff that her house seemed suspended on, that overlooked the beautiful lakeside and she started to share her rather sad story.

She was a widow. Her husband succumbed to a mental disorder that took his life. I did not ask how, and she did not offer. He left her house and property rich, but economically poor. She was humble and you could tell did not have much to sustain herself. She did angel card readings for a living and has a son. He was in his bedroom and did not come out the whole time I was with her. He also suffers from a mental illness and does not work out of the house. She displayed a matter-of-fact demeanor and did not complain about her situation. She even seemed kind of calm and peaceful. She did not ask for anything, in fact she had gifts for me.

She led me back into her living room and did an angel card reading for me that was very accurate. Then she made me a cup of tea, sat me down on her worn, but much-loved couch, with a couple of biscuits and a VHS tape she plopped into a worn-out machine. She said "just watch this. Please be open and I will be back in forty-five minutes".

What happened next changed my life. It was the very first time I watched the documentary *The Secret*. I have since watched it many times and read all the books. That first time was like an inner light was about to illuminate. This video was the manifestation of all the desires of my heart and soul. The choices I made to take my life in a new direction were solidified. The seeds had been planted and were starting to grow. I loved it; the whole concept was brilliant. It felt like an opening, or like some sort of internal baptism was happening in this stranger's home. She opened her heart, her home, and her arms to me. She gave me three more VHS copies and said, "Please spread *The Secret* to as many who will listen and heed the messages". She then walked me out to my car and refused the money I offered her to buy some food. But then I remembered I had the extra food from my daughter's party. I opened my trunk, without knowing what food my daughter had placed inside it. I handed the sweet, kind, lady three bags of fresh buns and two bags of fully cooked fresh fish. She took the food and returned to her doorway, waving, and possessing a deep smile, suggesting a safe trip home. Yes, I too teared up all the way home thinking about the exact same thought you are all having. How Jesus fed the hungry crowd loaves of bread and fish. I never saw her again, but I will never, ever, forget my first, second, third and fourth vision board and the place they were first born from.

It's early morning again, and I can't seem to sleep. This book is being summoned and created from all sorts of emotions that are keeping me from my deep sleep. I am a deep sleeper for the most part. I think it's because I am, most times, a very early riser. I was sharing healing energy with a powerful insightful healer, a woman who lights up the world. She is an agent acting as a light worker, mother, wife, ambassador. She knows who she is, and I will keep her private for her own sacredness. But I just wanted to say, as I shared with her my thoughts about spreading love from heaven. She lit up like a Christmas tree and smiled, her shinny eyes glossing over, explaining in that very moment she had a vision of me in this cape. She said like a superhero, spreading huge balms of healing love showering them everywhere. I shared this with my editor, who is also an artist, and created the cover of my last book, *Coming out of Darkness*. The idea and cover for this book will be created out of these musings of our passionate brainstorming. A showering of stars from heaven, with likely an abstract figure of a women sitting on the top of a mountain range, over a city of lights in the darkness. Sitting silently and quietly as everyone still lay sleeping. Showering them with love balms from heaven. I think, for now, I can literally tuck myself back under the covers and try to sleep for another couple of hours. The sky is just starting to take the thick dark shadow of the night off its' back. I feel like this is what I was awakened for, and this is what was needed to be said. I always remember my mothers' words when this happens, and I am called into God service. She says, "You can sleep when you're dead". She is funny that way, always has a metaphor; she is very witty and extremely funny. My mom is right though, sometimes you must listen to what is calling you and act upon the calling. So, I say to all of you, make for yourself the best day possible. As the sun comes up and you're sipping on your coffee, take a moment to spread some love from heaven and sprinkle it, like the sugar in your coffee. Every single moment of living doesn't stop. It's contagious, it catches on and it will make a difference in the moments you choose to live, in love, in lives and in each other.

Cayenne Pepper and Queen Anne's Lace

Recently, I took nineteen glorious days to have a real vacation. It felt like I was about to be gifted something special as we drove our RV motorhome and headed out. Excited to explore from different perspective, as the large windows and height of the motorhome provided us a higher place to see our surroundings. As we drove along Canada's eastern coast, through the hills and mountains of New Brunswick and Nova Scotia, I was in awe of the raw, inhibited, yet natural beauty. It was a wild God Garden full of valleys, waterways, green vegetation, fields of wildflowers, purple clover, and handfuls of Queen Anne's lace.

I must admit, seeing the sights from the height of the RV window was like being at the movies. With the wide, expansive views, while perched on my seat, and feeling a bit regal. Like I had my very own window seat in an episode of *The Nature of Things*.

Seeing small towns nestled in the valleys, and tall trees stretching to reach the sun on the mountain tops. The vast amount of water stretching the Atlantic Sea shores and the incredible Northumberland Strait. The color of the Petitcodiac River, that weaves its' way out to the sea. In Moncton, New Brunswick, the color reminded me of chocolate milk. It is brown because of the siltation and tidal forces. Siltation happens when fine particles of soil wash downstream. Much of the natural soil in the area has reddish brown color to it, explaining the color that reminds me of chocolate milk, making it's' way to the sea.

Looking at life, perched on my seat, as we drive further east to our destination of Prince Edward Island. It has been breathtaking, nerve racking, and exhilarating. Joe has been the person doing all the driving. He is an exceptional driver, but driving this thirty-six-foot motorhome, there have been some very challenging moments. Especially when the GPS seems to take us off the highway and down some steep and sketchy back hill roads, to avoid a fifteen-minute detour, claiming to be a quicker route to our destination. Let's just say there were times I was silently asking for some assistance from Archangel Michael to help Joe take the wheel and said a few Our Fathers and Hail Mary's for extra support.

We finally arrive at the bridge to Prince Edward Island, and we make our way across the thirteen-kilometer-long bridge. I have been on this bridge twice before, but in a car both times, so I could only see the cement wall that supports the structure of the bridge. This time it was like seeing the island coming towards us, with bright red clay fingers extending a welcome greeting. The tide was out, and as we got closer to the shore; you could see it stretching out along the Northumberland Strait. It was an emotional moment as I sat quietly feeling my roots, my ancestors, my family quietly calming me, calling me, welcoming me home. Something about the sea, widely chopping in all directions, the salt spraying, the smell of fish through the windows, and life residing in its' body lulls me home. It's a natural occurrence, embracing your soul, if you come from the seashore.

We arrive on the island, and, in a short twenty-eight minutes, I see my parents. My dad glancing at his watch as he has calculated the amount of time it should have taken us to reach Summerside from the bridge. I smile, some familiar things, like the gestures of your parents (if you are still lucky enough to have living parents) brings a happy, stirring to my soul. We have arrived. We spent a total of five days on the island. The first night we were tucked behind Lil and Irv's home. They are good family friends of my parents, who we also fondly love, and got permission from their landlord, Rosemarie, to stay one night. Our first campsite, for the next three nights, was called Twin Shores. It was another twenty-eight minutes to my parents' house in Summerside. It was breathtaking. You could see the ocean from one window and the Malpeque Bay from the other, it was a spectacular view. Yes, where the world famous Malpeque mussels everyone raves on about are from. I am not a mussel lover, but Joe really enjoys the way they are cooked in PEI. I save my taste buds for scallops, crab, and lobster. Yes, not a cheap date on an island dinner for me! I go for the top-notch eastern seafood, no bar clam casserole for me.

I fell in love with Twin Shores. It's a huge RV park that has a ton of activities, but for us it was a location to write, rest, and travel back and forth to my parent's home. Visiting, eating, catching up, and just being with my folks. What I really want to talk about in this chapter is Joe being smart enough to buy a little scooter big enough for the two of us to travel around on. It was fun to go back and forth down the country roads of PEI and dance with the wildflowers. The breeze, peppering the sides of the road, all embedded in sand the color of cayenne pepper. The purple thistles of my childhood, mixed with brown-eyed Susan's, all swam and played in the beautiful fields covered in Queen Anne's lace. This took my breath away, several times, as we traveled back and forth at least eight times from the campsite to their home. I loved the breeze, that almost blew us off the road, and the way the sun hit the flowers. But mostly I loved their slow dance with Divine, as if to say, "Thank you for making me and thank you for giving me such a beautiful place to live". I could have sworn on one sunset drive home that the fairies where having a party with the wildflowers, and Queen Anne's lace was holding court and hosting the event.

We did a lot of things together but mostly we just loved the time we got to spend together. When it was time to go, it was difficult for all of us to say goodbye. I felt blessed and heartbroken at the time, as we made our way back over the bridge. Starting out on our next leg of the journey. I did not want to spend a lot of time thinking about what I did not have, but rather what I had just been given, a gift. A visit with people I love, and a gift that I got to share it with my beloved Joe. Next, we traveled to a small town near Trenton and stayed overnight in a Walmart parking lot. I loved it. Being a newbie to RV traveling, it's kind of a common thing for RV people to stay at Walmart, in between destinations. We then arrived at my sister Kelly's home to visit, for a cup of coffee. She lives very near Trenton, as does her daughter Sarah. We got to meet my great nephew Oscar, who will be called Ozzie, and was just six days old. That was another highlight, it was a bonus visit. We traveled on and we ended up in a little town called Little Bras D'or. Joe found this cool campsite with a view that took my breath away. Arm of Gold was the name of the park. And I'm not kidding, the grounds were set up on a cliff that stretched over water. The islands and marshland seemed to have no beginning and no end. The breeze was always present no matter the time of day. We stayed here for three glorious days and nights. It was beautiful. I felt like I was living in heaven in some ways. I never wanted to leave. We explored the area, went for scooter rides along the shores, up and around the Cabot Trail, and mountains that extended views. I did not know it existed. It was fantastic, surreal, and exhilarating.

When we left, I noticed, all along our journey of the entire east coast, that Queen Anne's lace was with us in the fields on the side of the road, cliff views, and ditches. She was everywhere. Waving with grace, extending a personal invitation to be one with her. In her presence, in her home, slow dancing in the eastern breeze with her, in the peppered cayenne that sustained her life.

Slow Dancing With the Patina of My Parents

Joe can be the sweetest guy; he knows my parents live quite a distance from me and he also knows I am not one to ask for a lot. We decided we wanted to take some time away from work. His work, my work, and do a drive vacation in our (new to us) RV. We had a couple of "test" weekends away, for Joe to get familiar with how it operates. We set out for the longest vacation we have had yet together, a total of nineteen days. Today, we are exactly in the middle of our vacation time. It has been lovely for the most part. A bit nerve wracking for some of the hills (we did not expect to climb) and a few of the big bumps that jostled things around inside. But for the most part it has been breathtaking and heart changing. Today for example, we are staying at an RV camp called the Arm of Gold. It is the closest campground to the Newfoundland ferry, in a little town called Little Bras D'or, Nova Scotia. They also have on site, the most mouth-watering, homemade, crinkle cut French fries I have ever tasted. It is as if God came down and painted this view of the inlet from the Atlantic Ocean. I feel I have a front row seat at the most scenic landscape a person could ever hope to see. It only costs fifty dollars a night to stay here; for hydro, water, and sewer. It's a glorified hotel on wheels, with my very own little house on a hill. We got up, had our coffee, breakfast, set out on the scooter, crossed the bridge, and followed the shore along this stretch of water, viewing homes high up in the hills. Stretching for miles, settled on the cliffs. Then we crossed the highway, and climbed the mountains, finding our way home. It was magical. We stopped for a homemade bowl of turkey soup at a little diner nestled along the inlet shore.

We arrived back to our little home on wheels. Joe was tinkering, I was reading, and then I felt the familiar itching of my fingers searching for my computer. Calling for me to write about my parents, as it is still fresh in my mind. Allowing the bruising of leaving them, two days ago, to rise to the surface. I want to honor them in a way I never have before but wanted to let the emotions settle and for my vision to be clear, so I can write what I need to say to them and what I want to tell the world. My father will be eighty-six on August 29 and my mother will be eighty-three on November 16th. My father wants to see the Bluenose for his birthday, which I believe they are trying to arrange for him. It's a magnificent ship, formally used for fishing and racing and became a provincial icon for Nova Scotia in the 1930s. In celebration of the ships' 100th birthday, it is making its' rounds on the eastern harbors. My dad would love to see her, so my mother was planning with their dear friends, who are like family. They visit back and forth every day. Seeing my mom last week took my breath away, she held me and looked deeply into my eyes and kissed my face. It brought me back to all the years she did just that, wiped away my tears, my pain, and raised me to believe I was made of good things. My mom had a hard time showing emotions when I was growing up but as she aged and softened, so did her heart like a fine dusting of patina. I called this chapter Slow Dancing with the Patina of My Parents for this exact reason. I can see them now for all they were, all they experienced, sacrificed, and all they tried to do for everyone who ever meant something to them.

As I sat in her home and watched her fuss, work, gather, create, bake, and sedate us all, the only way my mother truly ever knew how to do. She did this to show her love, to create food, and lots of it. She had made soups, biscuits, cabbage rolls, cookies, the list

64

went on. In the five days we spent with my parents, she never stopped. She literally danced around her oven, her stove, her kettle, her coffee pot. She never stopped moving. Despite her four-foot ten frame (she will argue with you that she is five feet, but never has been), she talks and walks like a giant most of the time. I smile as I think how the younger generation would be put to shame by my mother's tireless energy. Watching her with pride, I started to familiarize myself with her dance steps. Side-stepping out of the way, grabbing a tea towel, washcloth, hot potholder, or a place mat, stepping in time as to not disturb her actions of love. Her display of pride, as she nourished our hearts, bodies, and souls. I found her rhythm without disturbing her and I felt good that I was able to dance with the best part of her. She makes me proud in a way that I can't describe, but it seeps out of my eyes and trickles down my cheeks. She grabbed my hand and dragged me out the door to all her neighbors, to share with them her eldest baby. We laughed and shared as we got to know each other. It made my heart burst open when she had me run plates of her homemade food, and luscious desserts, to the women next door. Every time we sat down to eat; Marie got to share with us. I love the bond my mother has with her neighbors. It is sacred and special, in a sisterly friendship kind of way. My mom is very shy, so to see her beam with that sparkle, and laugh at secret jokes with these women, warms me up. It lets me know she has happiness and real, honest, caring people in her life, when we all live so very far from her. I wanted my mom to have a day off so I suggested before we came that she finds a place where we could have a spa day together. She was on a hunt and her other neighbor across the way, Sally (yes, I was also dragged across the street and introduced to Sally) told my mom about this little shop across the field had just opened. That is where my mom and I spent the entire afternoon, on the last day of my visit. My mother's very first pedicure and manicure. She loved it so much that my sisters and I will never let my mother go without one again. The owner was so kind to my mother, and I could see my mother was tucking the shop owner into her heart and adopting her. My mother since then has baked them peanut butter cookies and dropped them off. Of course, she has, she knows no other life but service. Slow dancing with my momma was etched on my heart and will forever be a gift of timing, maturity, wisdom, laughter, and good food. My mom is my hero and the one person who taught me by her actions, not her words, how to love someone. Without words she taught me full on examples of untampered, unconditional, raw love.

My father, on the other hand, is a wild card. A story that deserves all kinds of verbiage, history, and nostalgia. My father is a storyteller, who, is good at yes, telling stories. Maybe that is where some of my writing comes from. He is intense and passionate. A man who is not always compassionate, as he is a scientist by birth and by nature. I found this out on an even deeper level on this trip, than I ever allowed myself to go. My father is supersonic sensitive, wise, honest, kind, truthful, and as we all are, selfish. My father is my mother's world; my mother is my father's world. This is what I have most remembered, as their growing pains over the years Criss crossed into, and around, each other's lives. My father always felt called to service. I can remember as a young girl my father's obsession for knowledge, creativity, exploration, and wonder. My visit with my pappy, as I call him, was gentler this time. It was like I had erased all the things I felt I needed to let go of, that were personal between us over the years. For my own internal and external healing and deep forgiveness. I came without an agenda, or chip on my shoulder, or a need to be heard or understood. I came to see my parents with an open heart and a blank piece of paper to write a new story on. It was beautiful. My father, pappy, had some very kind things to say to me and he expressed how proud he was of me several times in our time spent together. We talked about his scientific brain and his need for proof. The differences between us are so vast, as I have no need for scientific proof. I just believe in all the wonders that I get to witness, without one shred of scientific proof. He seemed to be in awe of that gift that I hold in the center of my world. My father is very religious and goes to mass often, but I'm not sure if he relates to the same spirituality as me. Deep inside my nature are the connections I have with Spirit. My father loves God, the trinity, and follows the doctrine of the Roman Catholic faith to the letter. I have a different form of practice but still feel at home in any church. We differ in a way that unites and intrigues, forming a genuine respect for each other.

My father asked me, on the morning of the last day of our visit, if I would accompany him at the cemetery to visit family that has passed on. He took my hand and we walked into where my Grandmother Bella, Grandfather Ernie, Auntie Carmella, and my Uncle Dennis were laid to rest. We spent some time reading the information on the tombstones. I learned that my uncle Dennis, my father's brother, passed away when he was an infant baby boy, just eight months old. My auntie passed and was buried with her parents. She was a lovely auntie, I really enjoyed knowing her. She lived with us in Ontario, for one summer, when she first came to visit. She ended up moving close by for many years, until after my grandfather passed away. She moved back home to take care of my grandmother. I felt an overwhelming desire to sing, and I asked my pappy if he would mind. He held my hand as we sang together How Great Thou Art. I then proceeded to say a prayer, asking my family to meet my pappy, when it was his time to go home to be with all of them. We, together, still holding hands, danced a slow quiet dance connected in this memory of love together. Tears misted our glasses and filled our hearts with this wonder in the moment of interconnection, flesh, father, daughter, and Spirit.

We quietly got back in the car and drove over to the new area were my parents bought their cremation plot. I thought it might give me goosebumps to read the tombstone and see the plot. It did not, instead it empowered me to sway with my father, hand in hand, dancing to the energy and the pride he had in showing his oldest child the place where he and his beloved will be laid to rest together. It was a modest headstone, a black onyx, heart-shaped stone. He said mommy preferred that it was simple yet elegant. Like the dance I used to watch them sneak in together, on a Sunday night after dinner, on the living room hardwood floor. My father was a very good dancer. We held hands and did not speak. I bent down and noticed it read what was written on the bottom, "Together Forever". Simple, yet two words holding so much power. I said a prayer that they would be blessed and protected and that the one leaving first, would be the one returning, to bring the other one home. That they would always be there for each other in flesh, and then reunited in spirit and eternally bound. My father had a lump in his throat and managed to squeak out "You're good at this kiddo". It was a huge compliment, but what was even richer was the peace that seemed to flood his body and land on his face.

We arrived back to his home, had coffee and freshly baked cookies from a tin my sweet momma placed on the table from her freezer. We sat for another half hour. I started feeling anxious, that if I did not get up and rip off the Band-Aid and say my goodbyes my heart would literally explode at the kitchen table, breaking into a million pieces on my mother's tiled kitchen floor. Her friend Lillian says it best, "You can stay an hour, a day, a week. It's all going to hurt the same when you say your goodbyes, so best just get it over with". My mother held me tighter than she ever has, looked deeply into my eyes, and professed all kinds of love, in action, tears and words. She whispered in my ear the promise of this hug again, as the good Lord was not ready for her yet. I held my breath and tried to be brave, failing miserably. My heart ached inside its' cavity, and I can only imagine the ache that echoed mine in hers. My father was the same. Kind eyes, worn with the patina of time, deeply blue, deeply grateful, full of love and promised of another time we could be together again. We left, all of them waving blowing kisses. Tears streaming down my cheeks, Joe sitting silently in the driver's seat keeping it together. I could feel his love, his quiet strength, allowing me the space of one final slow dance. The memory of my parents, getting smaller and smaller, as we drove down the road to the bridge that brings us back home. She made sure, as always, to send food with us. We took soup, cabbage rolls, fresh homemade buns, and cherry cheesecake for the journey. I am one lucky little girl, as an adult woman, to have what I have in my parents. Two people who are still living large, loving large, laughing large, and eating large.

Befriending Experience

Awareness, when drenched in silence, takes on a whole new voice, depending on what kind of mental equation you might be giving energy to. I learned to take timeouts from my crammed life, and to really focus on some stubborn patterns. What's interesting is, in the silence they can't hide in distractions, or activities.

Some patterns, I've realized throughout this process of diving deep and taking time to address them, have turned out to be patterns that I have chosen to keep. Keeping them and defining them help me maintain stability, accountability, routine, and everyday responsive actions. Allowing for a healthy mind, body, soul existence.

The routine that always starts my day is a perpetual pattern of waking up around seven am, six out of seven days a week. This pattern helps me get my day set, organized, and all the appointments aligned. It starts, most days, with Joe and me having a quiet coffee and a light breakfast. He reads the news of the day and I do some mindless tasks while still waking up. As the day moves on, the patterns of my life loop from one hour to the next, creating a routine that can change, and does change often.

I chose the word "befriend" on purpose for the title of this chapter and felt the need to elaborate on why we as humans choose patterns. I feel we use routine and patterns to help us feel like we have at least some kind of accountability. To keep us in perpetual motion, feeling some sort of value, both internally and externally.

Routines, such as jobs, which provide an income that helps us sustain life. A life that houses us, feeds us, helps us build security or savings. Allowing us the opportunity to explore extracurricular activities, other forms of stimulation or experiences, are so important to the growth of most people. This all equates to structure and patterns of a habitual routine that takes up space in our day, and time in our lives.

Coming to terms with making friends, with some of the rituals and patterns that co-create your unique existence, can be challenging at the best of times. My current job, working for Source, was something I tucked away in the very back corner of my brain for several years. Taking time to learn from all sorts of modalities and masters, of divine and spiritual sources. Over the course of several years I would study, take courses, and work on the start of my degrees. My path was taking a different direction, as the rest of my life was led in a more traditional form of making money. Being responsible to sustain a sufficient flow of it, but also allowing me to pave my way through life. I think now as I look back over all the jobs, life skills, hardships and wear and tear on my being, how much patience it took, waiting for the perfect job to form. Paying the prices, I did in the experiences. Splitting my time, learning new skills, along with my life lessons.

Almost everyone you strike up a conversation with has a history they are quite willing to share with you, a story or two that makes them either laugh or smile while telling it. Most people want to talk about life in general, what they have learned or been challenged by, inspired, or simply just want a chance to talk about things that seem important to them. It's how we invest in people, how we find our tribe some would say. They spent a lot of time finding people who would accept them, where they fit in, where they felt understood, a connection.

Sometimes we need to step out of the patterns we are stuck in and take a chance to find another way to realign the stagnation that has settled into our being. To remove the comfort of ordinary and simple and change up our patterns. This may seem like a simple thing to accomplish but it is one of the hardest things to put into action, to be honest. Finding space in quiet to step out of the path you have carved out in this world is easier said than accomplished. By the time most people reach a point in their life, where they find themselves without the responsibilities that were chosen in their younger years (career, children for example), they are well into the second half century of their life. In most cases, people find they are more tired than they were in their early twenties when they were choosing these lifelong commitments. So, if you're not flexible with letting go of very old patterns, you may never get to experience the meaning and true worth of freedom. Freedom to explore the things you only dreamed about, freedom to discover that no one is ever too old to discover a new pattern of life, and the beauty it may sustain your soul in.

As I have suggested, this is not my first choice of career. However, in choosing this career I get to choose freely because the other careers led me to a place, this life, this world of unconditional love. In saying this, I had to find unconditional love in all my other jobs to end up at this life purpose. It is a process. Addressing my needs and sticking to a course of consistent patterns or the routine they presented.

A bit of personal history here, I started working as a babysitter when I was about 12 years old. Back in my day there was an actual babysitting course you could take. It was held at the fire department in our little town; at the end of the course, you had to write an exam to pass. If I remember correctly, it was very much safety orientated, understandably. It was my first job, which led to quite a bit of babysitting, sometimes even over weekends. My second job, which I truly detested, was picking asparagus. We got picked up by a farmer at 5:30 am, a man who did not speak one word of English. He was Hungarian and tough as nails. Each day he dropped us off in a wet, cold field. The dawn was always just crusting through the dirt when we arrived each morning. It was cold, wet, uncomfortable work, and it the pricks hurt my young hands. But it was something that I accepted and was expected of me; to earn a living for the extra things I wanted, not needed, that my parents could not afford. How could I know way back then that this job would teach me so many lessons of gratitude? At the time, I can certainly and honestly attest that I was not the least bit grateful. Most mornings I felt in utter despair of having to do this awful summer job.

This foundation of my early years molded me, saved me, dug me out of the dirt as my life found bump after bump, loss after loss. I do not share this history of my life with you to gain sympathy, I share this because befriending hardships creates internal kryptonite. This strength prepared me in the way that nothing that came after ever took me out of the living for very long, bouncing me back to pick another course, another lesson.

I have had several careers and jobs during my lifetime. Sometimes doing double or triple duty, shifting between several jobs at once. This hard work taught me an incredible work ethic. My jobs, the interaction, the pain, the frustrations, the physical exhaustion taught me that hard work and routine can befriend you. I know this may sound strange or even unrealistic but, let me try to explain this theory a bit deeper.

It was in my last seventeen-year career, out in the work force that was my biggest life lesson. Ironically, I worked most of the last six years in complete solitude, for three quarters of my workday, every single day, five days a week. I am sure you have heard it said more than once (or hundreds of times, as I have), nothing in life is a coincidence. When you are ready to receive the lesson in the experience, it just unfolds. This part of my life was no exception, in fact, the incredible touching experience has allowed me to take on my current job, and working for Source with the wisdom and truth it requires to do the work.

I had worked for my previous job, in a very big building close to my home. In fact, I could walk to work most days. It took all of five minutes, as it was just two blocks from home. It was a beautiful atmosphere of camaraderie and customer service. Several of us all worked very closely in the main office part of the building. A narrow hallway filled with a long row of cubicles. There were two full time receptionists, and I was one of them. My co-worker was witty, and we had the life. Let me tell you, every day I pretty much loved going to work for this company. Things change, they always do, and some corporate management decisions were made. New people moved into existing positions, and the dominoes started to fall, bringing many casualties with it, changing lives and routine. I felt uncertain for the next phase of my life. When the company relocated, my own job was changed in the biggest way and I struggled with fear, isolation and the long forty-five-minute commute. I lost sleep over this change. My brain would continually worry about all the "what if" scenarios this change could bring. One other huge change is that I would be facing my job alone, as they scaled back and only wanted one receptionist. My life was very unsettled on the inside, but I held a brave face and carried on hearing the little engine saying, "You can do this Tracey!"

As I settled into the huge, new space that was to be my home, for the next part of my work world, I remember feeling lonely in a way that was so heavy on my heart that my heart physically hurt in the middle of my chest, to the point it was concerning me. I felt completely isolated from my co-workers. The world I knew was gone and I was grieving it in a way I did not even understand. Talking to myself suggesting "You're being silly, stop it. You have a job; you have the most beautiful office in the whole building. It's huge and full of windows, that stream of steady sunlight, big blue skies, clouds, storms, and all the nature around you, what is the matter with you".

It took almost a year to identify what the problem was but eventually I was able to. I was alone, totally alone, in the biggest, forced paid silence of my entire career. I did see my co-workers every day as they bustled in together. Some took the stairs, some so laden down with work that they had to take the elevator. But it was a brief daily connection for about thirty minutes. I decided every single day to greet "my people". I called them this with the biggest smile I could muster, and the warmest wishes for their day. This also happened for thirty minutes every night from 4:30 pm to 5:00 pm. I decided to be in this divine frame of mind and heart. No matter what I was feeling, I gave them every ounce of love I could muster up. What happened was huge. Instead of feeling fear and loneliness, I felt the comfort of this new silence that had invaded my busy life with words, people, obsessions, noise. This silence started to become my very best, proactive friend.

In this huge gift of silence, which by the way I was being compensated for in a very generous way, became the backbone of who I am and what I represent in my life every day. This silence taught me to listen to the frustration of customers, who were dissatisfied with our product, seeking justice, and getting results. I was always so proud of how our company assumed responsibility for unhappy consumers. We always took care of the reputation of our company's name and made a bad situation a good outcome. I found a new sense of belonging in this silence, a space to make a difference. I learned to listen to the consumers who came through our front entrance, which was control locked. Not often, but they did come. I learned to listen instead of just hearing. It was a huge, humbling lesson to listen to understand and not judge a situation and the outcome. I was not always successful. If someone was a bully, or rude, or felt entitled, sometimes that made me like a defensive prickly pear, but I did learn to settle down those ruffles of self-righteousness.

All of this was the Divine honing his child, preparing her for her last career, preparing her in a way she had no idea about, and could not know at the time, what he had planned for her. I took several years (the last five to be exact) to build on this silence, befriend it, saturate the experience into all the layers of my life. Using this silence taught me to listen, forgive, and find internal responsibility. My boss, who was (and I am sure still is) an earth angel in disguise. She totally understood the need for what I could offer, in the environment I was working in. The solitude of the space was a haven for troubled co-workers to come and sit beside me and iron out a thing or two. My boss not only allowed this behavior to happen, as sort of a counseling session, she supported it and allowed the flow of Spirit to shift many into a positive space. In turn, allowing me to grow spiritually, in a surprising way, that it started to flow naturally. I have come to understand, deeply, that Divine Spirit always knows what Spirit is intending for us. I asked my boss if I could, in my silence while holding down the fort on the front lines, start investigating motivational things like watching Ted Talks, taking motivational online seminars, to enhance my customer service and to communicate the wisdom I was receiving. She of course said "Yes, whatever you think will help you adjust, please apply it". I think I stopped counting after one hundred Ted Talks, I watched several interviews on Own network, and took several self-motivational courses. These were inspirational and taught me, in the middle of my silent, lonely crisis, to make use of my time management in the best way. Silence can teach a person by being positively pro-active with the time, developing a higher frequency of positive energy.

There is value in accepting open, honest silence in the deep abyss. Quiet silence taught me and led me here today, working diligently for Divinity. This whole acceptance of something so very uncomfortable led me to the grace of silence. This grace of silence fills my life with powerful signs. I did not even see the signs in the distraction of noise. This awakening of light consciousness consistently fills the holes in my hurt. Once I made friends with the silence, I was elevated, integrated, to higher nonverbal frequency; communication that can only truly be heard in the silence it fills.

Befriending the lessons has allowed the experience of the lesson to lay new, strong foundations for my life, and in the leading of my lessons in facilitation. When channeling Spirit for others to find their passions, leaving behind the distraction and the pain, scar tissue and drama that sucks their energy and darkens their conscience. If I can help anyone that is stuck in a pattern or loop, seek clarity and healthier air, to escape their toxic environment, it is my responsibility to share all I have been taught and all that has allowed me to move on in enlightenment. Befriending my experiences in all the lessons they taught has given me the history and the truth to share with anyone seeking. I encourage the warrior to awaken in you. I encourage you to let go, to seek your passions, address your history, and acknowledge things you were proud of and things you were not. Shedding what you no longer need to hold on to and thereby creating brand-new real estate, unchartered territory from which a new birth internally can arise within you. Be your own best friend, learn to count on yourself, forgive yourself, and respect yourself. Be proud of who you are and the warrior within.

Deflection Is Rejection

This chapter had me taking a deep breath and letting out the air very slowly, a controlled sigh. I would rather not dance around the elephant in the room (the title of this chapter) but to invite that big grey mammoth to sit down with me and have a cup of soothing ginger tea. Entertaining and inviting each other's presence to an old-fashioned tea party, where were sit down and discuss this together, in an intimate exchange of truth and communication. I am trying to find a way to be diplomatic at addressing distraction and the reaction to distraction. My friend, or should say "Sister of Divine", point blank refers to her distractions as "little piles of her", leaving pieces of her everywhere. In all honesty, don't we all have our own little piles and pieces scattered about, in some sort of sequential order? I suppose anyone looking in on all of this might assume or even suggest it as an attention disorder.

"What leads some of us, do you suppose oh wise grey elephant, to have to feel so obligated to be pulled in a gazillion directions?" Trying to take on every request made of us as an obligation and responsibility, so much so that is loaded up high on our already overflowing dinner plates. Yet, that is what most of us tend to do, shovel more things higher on the pile, so high that it keeps falling off the sides. "Big breath, just hold it in, and release it slowly", the beautiful grey elephant quietly says, batting her huge, big, brown eyes. "Just let it go honey and sip your tea". I let it go and I can feel the exhaustion drain from my body, seeping into the cushion I am meditating on. I choose to meditate in this moment that could easily extend into thirty bliss-filled moments of peace and quiet. Resulting in the avoidance of the three loads of ironing, the unmade bed, and the basket of ripened peaches that could all use some of my attention.

Why do we feel guilty if the order of the tasks is not organized based on priority or does not align in a systematic way, like dominoes laid out and falling in an orderly fashion? What or who makes us feel this way? This deep, foreboding of guilt that floods in, disturbing the order or non-order of our lives. In this deep dive, addressing the deflection of disappointments, I have realized that it was a part of the way I was disciplined as a small child. That was, you were not useful unless you were doing for others. Either by helping in the homestead, chores, or working as a family unit. Idle hands were not of God or good. If you were idle at all you were deemed lazy or selfish. This is the foundation of my generation and several ones before me. Labor was intense, back breaking and had a place of honor.

This new world, the world of fast-paced everything; robotic replacements of human bodies even the mathematics of automation, has literally given us the ability to find more personal pockets of time in our day, to be more personally proactive. More time to develop skills, write, and journal, read articles, exercise, learn new recipes, and delve into spiritual gifts. I can remember not so very long ago when it took two full days for my mother to do the laundry in our household, every single week, and it was an eight-hour day of full-on labor. Washing, hanging to dry and then a full day of ironing. We have a different life now, as we live it in the twenty-first century, and technology has freed up our time.

Why, then, do we still have so many unfinished little piles of things we cannot get to, things we shove into closest, drawers, pile on shelves, we cannot or do not want to tackle? Projects we start on in a full-on sprint, only to discover two weeks later it's tucked away in a drawer that we had forgotten where we had put it in. Why do we struggle so much, trying to solve all our thoughts? Why do you think we struggle with disconnection, oh wise grey mammoth friend? People, as a majority, are not able to focus on finishing most things. Constantly being distracted by the next great life-changing idea that they feel for certain is going to change the world.

For me, this is about my own distraction. My reaction commonly turns to deflection, allowing me to justify my next thought. Focusing and justifying the importance is greater on the lined-up agenda, my day takes order in.

Order is a burden. For most people it takes time to step out of the rat race, looping, and consistent noise of responsibilities that shout at you like a sergeant, demanding consistency, and accuracy on the firing range of life. It barks out what should be done next, and most times the voice is loud and overshadows the artistic softness that sparks your unique identity. This order comes from rules that have been passed down from century to century, stating the rules to live and love and support are mandated by common sense. Yet the creative side of you gets hungrier and hungrier, as it is seemingly always the last one to be fed at the table of life.

In all honestly, we do not allow our tired, routine-led bodies much of a break or a timeout to just be quiet in the silence our bodies need to recover in. I have discovered, in this quiet reflection on this chapter that this is what I have done for years, deflect what I can't seem to bite off or finish. In this reflection, I have been able to release the hundreds of promises and projects I was never able to finish and start over in a brand-new mindset. How have I been able to get on top of this? I stopped running, did a massive spring cleaning, and did not load those same shelves up with unfinished thought patterns. I have come to honor my time and what kind of energy I allow to take up residence with my time that helps balance it all out. I think through every single pile, theory, thought, placing it in a sequence of importance. I make lists now that keep me accountable and a time frame around the idea or thought on the list. The biggest change is that I don't take on more than I can handle, as far as deadlines. I have two distinct lists that incorporate, in a practical order, as far as the needs and responsibilities in my day. What does my soul need to have fun and smile, and what are my responsibilities?

When I used to deflect the chaos I created, all the disorder would nag at me and cause me a delay in finding a whole sense of silence and order. Keeping me stuck, like standing in clay or mud would, it acted as a deterrent. Like swimming upstream and not able to produce any momentum. All this did to me, and for me, was to cause more frustration and have less productive fuel to move on in my daily life. Deflection, I quickly found, when I took some timeout in silence and quiet to rebuild this old pattern, was reminding me I was rejecting my true nature, and all the wisdom, gifts, and productivity I could accomplish. Because I took the timeout to address these unfinished piles, I was able to create new momentum and honor the piles I needed to address, close out, release, and give away. This makes these piles easier to maintain and easier to understand. The understanding allowed me to resurface and join life with all the gifts I have to offer. When I was rejecting myself there was no movement, there was no way I could help anyone as I had no idea how to unbury myself from the piles I never got to, put them to bed, or finish, so I could start a new project.

One might ask "Is this easy?" My answer is nothing worthwhile, or habit forming, is ever easy. It takes energy to stop, and to slowly look at the reconstruction that may be redirected within. Everything life changing and worthwhile, must first be developed internally, before it can be put into practice. And all these changes, yes all of them, require stopping and making new choices. The old ways have outlived their purpose, or the routine has changed. Due to the growth, responsibilities have shifted, and you have not yet caught up with the changes. Children require all your attention and time as they grow, but when they grow, in most cases it's hard to let go. So, you continue to invest in them in a way they do not need you to invest in them anymore. We get stuck and stagnant in this and sometimes the conflict is hard, and we gain weight or form unhealthy addictive behavior patterns as we continue to stay around in places that all of us have quite simply outgrown. Little piles of frustration build up and you are trapped in a place you don't know how to separate from, causing a dependency that is not healthy between you and your child. This is just one example of deflecting the truth, to take care of yourself in a way that is required for you to gain back your full purpose, as well as allowing your child to learn adult responsibility and accountabilities.

Little piles of accomplishments can cause more stress internally than you are even consciously aware of. Take the time for reflection, to address what you may be keeping yourself from. Take the time to learn what is in your piles, what uses they may still have for you, for your growth, for the advancements you want to make, or the lessons you want to proceed with giving your full attention to. Changing life patterns takes hard work. You must be ready for the pain that might occur as you detach from some situations that are not healthy, or that you may be enabled by or are the enabler for, in each other's relationships.

Deflection is rejection. Truly, there is no kinder way to put these two words together and the meaning of them when teamed up together. It's a self-sabotaging of not being enough, for all the lifelines that are connected to your core, your heart, your soul. You are enough! You are enough to take charge and change the course and the direction of your life, providing a place of pure bliss. You have the power to sweep up those piles, addressing the importance and order by which they align personally, and passionately for you. Take the time you need to align, reconstruct, and form a new internal personal constitution that vibrates in the healthiest way possible. Take on you, take on the things that bring music to your words, which resonate and vibrate along with your internal engine, aligning in time with the beating of your physical heart. You are worth it. I just looked at the clock, its eleven-eleven, this makes me smile. A small voice says to the center of my heart "It's time to spend the rest of your day rejoicing in nature, catching lunch with Joe, walking in the park. It's time to tackle another small pile of Tracey and change the course of it. It's time to know you are blessed, and Divine has you covered on all angles. It's time to accept every single flaw in you and push rejection in the ditch that is covered with fall wildflowers. It's time to breathe in and release the nagging little sadness of the past that keeps trying to push you in the ditch with the rejection". So happy to be here today and experience what life is bringing me. Bring it on! As for my big grey mammoth, thank you for joining me for tea, reflection, acceptance, and your wisdom. Your silent strong presence fills me with refreshing air, bursting my lungs, ready to tackle yet one more day. A new pile to place in order, in the disorder, of my lifelong living.

The Formula of Releasing

People that come for healing, who are seeking to address what they struggle with, are always asking what can I do to release all that is not serving a purpose. Sometimes, it's easy when you put two heads together, with spiritual direction, when a person knows what they need to release and how to address the releasing. There are other times when someone is so congested, lost, and misunderstood with themselves they just want to run for the hills and have zero desire to release what they cannot even identify. It's fearful trying to figure out what your next move is, in a world that has very little direction these days. To harmonize life, what we need to sustain our health, our governing of Ccuntries, our educational system, nutrition, and the poverty we suffer, not only personal, but the poverty of the state of our fractured emotional system has a million opinions on the best approach to varying degrees of wellness and solid practical solutions.

I spend many waking hours releasing as much as possible, in many ways. Let's talk about the physical ways to release. The routine and the formula that is assisting me may very well apply to you, if what I'm about to share with you feels good to you. I start as many days as possible with a positive attitude. Let me explain that, as I say this, my positive attitude does not mean that I am that person that jumps for joy with the energy of friendly bulldog, or with the exuberance that goes with the energy of someone who has already had three cups of coffee and are ready to charge the day. That is not me. Sometimes for the first hour after waking I do not feel like I even need to speak. However, my heart is full of love, life, and wonder. I am interested in things, and most times Joe banters on about these realities. I catch the snippets that matter to me and let the rest go. I never lose my appreciation for being alive, gaining a new day, and having my morning coffee. For me, this formula starts my day on the right foot and a clear perspective, creating renewed activity, setting a course for positivity in motion. This positivity leaks into my day, starting from the simple notion of bringing peace and joy to others. Allowing peace and joy to flow through me, and around me, this action of energy affirms for me often, as I get to connect to others seeking the same enlightenment.

Making time for others is another formula I employ. As an example, making Joe breakfast. Most of my days begin by being in service for others, starting with Joe. Not because he is the man of the house, or his job is more important than mine, or even has to do with him being the bigger bread winner. It has to do with service. Service of the heart, service to another person that makes them feel loved and cared for. This service, when you start your day by giving, tends to trickle into the rest of your day like a slow steady stream of sweet syrup, sticking to your ribs. Reminding you what it means when you are called to service. Even the tiniest gestures of service, and the consistency in doing them, forms incredibly important, repetitive, healthy habits. This is so important to setting the tone of your day and the routine you begin to incorporate. It's not just the service however, it's the feeling you release of love, not obligation that sets the formula you are trying to co-create with love and Divine essence. Expressing yourself with these little gesture's, such as making breakfast with love and a light heart, touching the hand of the person you love and taking a moment to let it settle in, smiling with the sparkle you have for that person in your eyes, teaches you that this works. If you continue the pattern, the routine forms inside of you, making it impossible to deliver breakfast any other way but with love in your actions and in your heart.

Releasing stagnant old energy that takes up a toxic space can be very difficult to detect. This energy tends to hide in pain, blocking anything that might have any power in wiping it out of your body, for short periods of time, or even forever. By releasing toxins, that may have otherwise clouded your perspective, and bringing new lightness to you instead, sends the darker side of energy into a state of confusion mixed with fear. This reminds the darker energy that it may not even be around to co-exist in a body that has chosen to live mostly in the light. Awareness is the tool, the formula, to create sustainable longevity of light within you. Add in truth, with a splash of peace and allow the ingredients to mingle, bubble, and dance within. This combination starts the engine of connected body and soul, delivering a space of freedom to recover in.

What is the process to release stagnant dark scar tissue and unwanted wounds? How to we understand what it is we need to release? How do we identify what is hurting us? How do we trust this formula of releasing will even work? Let's address one question at a time in this chapter to drive home the power of releasing.

To understand what it is we need to release means we must be open enough allow what is stuck, to surface. Most people think we must know what it is we are releasing, to release it. I don't believe this is true, at least in my experience. The releasing is an act of trusting there is a place of sacred space, where whatever was stuck in me, in either my past or present has a place, and I can trust that place, surrender, and release it. Sometimes we don't know what kind of energy we may be releasing; it isn't always white light. I do not want any harm to befall on anyone if the energy is not white light intended. Another part of me feels like I need to hold on to things sometimes, to honor the lesson, or to keep myself from repeating the same lesson. Hence, having difficulty releasing fully, so as I do not forget what I have learned in the lesson. Trust is the most important element and the whole entire answer to this question. We must trust the source we are releasing this sacredness to and know that the energy that is holding space and time for us will honor our lessons. Allowing space internally and making room for new ones to surface, or unfold, in our growth.

To identify what is hurting us we need to be open and allow the hidden scars to soften. Unearthing a memory that releases the feelings associated with the memory, gives us the knowledge that must come up and out of your karmic records, from past and present life. The healer or facilitator might be able to sense, see or feel in their mind's eye the knowledge that needs to be exposed to you. They will help to then release this stuck situation. Sometimes the clarity that presents itself is a surprise to you and something you did not realize you needed closure over. Once released you need to forgive the action, words, betrayal, or whatever the reason for being stuck is, whether it was administered by you or to you. Both ways must be forgiven and released from within you. It's been my personal experience, during healing sessions, when things do surface, there is no way I can deny it because the memory vision, and feelings are crystal clear. Sometimes even frame by frame I witness the act, or the memory with such clarity, I can see it without emotion and remember the details like it was happening again, only I am a witness not a victim.

We trust this process of releasing will work by going through the process of healing. I like to have healing sessions, for myself, with light workers who I feel called to hire for a session of healing, or even sometimes we exchange our healing services. I like to feel that I am in a place of unconditional love and acceptance, so I seek these light workers out and we get to work on, and with each other. This is the only real way I can let all my guard down. All the blockages rise out from the cracks and crevasses, as they do like to hide, and by doing so, gain strength. Sometimes there is a lot of shame and disgust in the choices I've made, that are buried away inside my body. This releasing works because if you open your heart and arms, and allow the process of healing to work, you can feel it leaving. It hurts, yes, it's extremely uncomfortable, and it feels foreign. Sometimes it's a big presence of unclaimed, unhealed, past scared energy that does take up a considerable amount of space in our vessels. You literally feel the energy releasing from your body and you literally receive assistance from someone pulling it out for you. Either by using sound, presence, voice, or energy, you then get to breathe the residual toxins out of your body trusting in the releasing. When it is gone, trust me, you know because you can feel the new space that has been created in its place by feeling peace, light, warmth, acceptance, hope, and wholeness.

Trust this releasing of old, unwanted energy with your life. Allow your soul, your higher self, your intuitive internal whole, and tri-dimensional body to guide you. Love yourself. Incorporate truth, aligning with facts that work when you practice the art, and gift of releasing unwanted energy that is encapsulated, and trapped in your body. Experience new birth in the choices you have made in the process of finding the courage of true self love.

Actions Can Manifest Spiritual Endorphins

What I have come to discover, as I uncover the truth, much like unraveling a big ball of yarn in my own internal space, is that my actions cause a reaction of energy that either stunts my growth or allows my growth to manifest new life. I have discovered, through the releasing and the awareness of the action that happens in every single solitary moment of my living in consciousness, that every action has a course of reaction.

The word endorphin comes from putting two words together; endogenous meaning from within the body, and morphine, which is an opioid pain reliever. In other words, endorphins got their name because they are a natural pain reliever. Hence, the spiritual aspect and the angel perspective I am speaking from, in the writing of this chapter.

When I speak of actions in this context, I speak of being personally accountable for my actions in everyday living and interaction with other human beings. Including those I cohabitate, work, play, and banter with. New and old ways of living, releasing to make room for more interconnection with others, and the lessons they will eventually provide me.

Sometimes the lessons are more painful than others. Sometimes the natural flow of releasing can feel like a deep wound that has a hard time healing. For one reason or another it tends to linger in a toxic infection I don't quite understand. Some lessons are attached to past life, unresolved relationships that have not had an opportunity for closure, or the forgiveness required allowing the closure to happen. This is all about releasing so that one can come to understand the natural flow of spirit-filled endorphins. This occurs by inviting healing and loving guided light into your core. Clearing out the toxic scars, the lessons, feeling the pain, and working through the experience in the interaction of these lessons.

Let's discuss actions a little deeper, shall we. Again, I can only share from my experience and my perspective. When I choose an action that comes from a dark place of hurt, or unresolved pain it's sometimes surprising to me when something surfaces that still brings me feelings of desperation. A sense of feeling saddened, trapped, clouded thoughts, or even being triggered by the presence of energy in a person I may not have been around for some time in the physical sense. Let's dissect this a bit more as we unravel what I am trying to say about the lower frequency that still feeds off these emotions.

Sometimes, I am not aware that I am repeating an action. A very deep, quiet, unresolved lesson that I did not have closure on. Something I did not even know was still an open wound. This happens when I am around an old relationship, a painful exchange of differences that were never talked about. This happened a lot with family members while I was growing up. Finding our way, and being a victim, or a bully in an encounter that was shoved deep down into my solar plexus.

The difference for me these days is that I am immediately aware of the details and the conversation that needs to occur between the conflict. Unblocking the pain with the new truth and the tools I have discovered. Having revealed the truth with the kindness in which it needed to be delivered. It is usually a conversation, a "let's get down to business" style of addressing and resolving the old, buried scars, and then releasing the energy to Spirit for disposal. I feel very fortunate that my Father in Spirit has loaded up my spiritual toolbox with a few new tools, to help release this energy, into a place I feel guided to releasing it. This action allows me to literally shake off the old stagnant energy that was feeding off, the energy I was not even aware I was giving it. Shaking it all away, allowing a vibrant flow of natural endorphins, to leave me shiny and transparent.

There is a win, win, double bonus factor in these actions. Especially if they happen to be immediate family members or relatives. I always say we don't really get to choose our families; we are born into the karmic contract our souls agreed to unite with before we became beings in the flesh. Meaning literally, we in our human vessels do not get to initially choose our path in flesh at the early stages of life but, we believe and have faith in our souls to settle this for us. We have agreed upon the contract to learn the next set of soul school lessons, before we come into bodily form. The lessons can be harsh and cause us to age in this vessel before it is our time. We can stop that decay by claiming the action, and the releasing, in the excruciating executions our bodies experience. Sometimes dying little by little in. Yes, by raising and releasing these toxins we receive natural, rejuvenating, spiritual endorphins. In general, I don't share what I have not personally had the experience in. So, I can attest to this new health, healing, and mindset giving me an abundance of healthy living. This causes my body to release, release, release. Toxic waste expelling out of me, allowing me to be free in this body to move around and experience the grace of peace in a whole new light.

I need you to be very aware of this next chapter. If this is the destiny, and the light work miracles you are seeking to claim for yourself, the action of your efforts will energetically attract others to this new awakening, and awareness. You must practice this every day. You must invite the white light, Father Spirit, the energy you belong too (and are not separate from) into your vessel. You must do this daily, as a new standard and quality of raising your vibration to relate to externally and internally, to this unconditional love. You then must practice, allowing this Source to help you release deeply what is NOT serving your highest good.

This is the secret I am sharing with you, that will bring on the natural spiritual endorphins you are seeking, for whole self. This is a gift, it is free, and you only need to have an open, truth-filled heart to ask for it. It's simply taking a deep breath, exhaling, and allowing what is not serving you to be released, and giving it the space to rest. Asking Source to help by connecting to you, and releasing this unwanted energy, trusting this releasing to source for disposal.

Manifesting a Picnic for One

We have discussed, throughout this book, the power words can have on perspective, views, and action. We have identified that it is our responsibility to manage ourselves through more productive and positive ways; to create healthy, habitual self-loving habits. There are many ways to fill all this new space that is created, once releasing has occurred. It seems to develop quickly in people looking for a different kind of internal structure. Positive enlightenment, growth, newly self-discovered awareness that affirms, and solidifies, the new real estate within. This invitation to absorb and marinate with Source allows for some new, fun, and creative opportunities.

Choosing my words carefully, around the subject of selfishness, reminds me exactly why I created the title of this chapter. I wanted to snag you, catch your attention, and then draw you in. Picnic is a word we usually connect to by recalling images of sharing food and time in nature, on some level, with special people we care about, love, and honor in a relationship. It is a time to experience a slowing down. Eating and drinking in a place that provides beauty and comfort in a setting like a park, waterfall, rock quarry, or beach; the list goes on and on. You can get creative and plan this as a family outing, a romantic reconnection with a lover, time with a friend, or group of friends that would celebrate this time with you. I would like you to think about setting all that normalcy aside, step inside your own unique space, and invite yourself on a picnic for one.

Many years ago, I was in a place that gave me the opportunity to start over. It was a time in my life when I was completely alone and needed to experience spiritual growth, and to release some residual pain. It was a three-year timeout without a partner. It took time to work through the quiet loneliness, to adjust to eating by myself. Cooking for one is not as fun as I thought it might be, but I quickly adapted to the loneliness by making my meals special. Enjoying the meals in places of beauty and changing the scenery as much as the season would allow, as often as I could. Sometimes the park, a beach, by the water, or on my balcony. It was important to me to have excitement and anticipation built around the meal presentation, in creating the picnic for one.

I took this to the next level that winter (not my favorite season) and created an elaborate space on my living room floor. Filling it with many blankets and pictures of the summer. This was my special place to eat food during the cold months, where I brought warmth to my body and a coziness to my space. This always made me smile with pure satisfaction. I never really shared (until now) how these picnics fed me and allowed me to develop an internal friendship in the quiet space and comfort of my home. It made me feel pride, pleasure, and confidence. It taught me that there is laughter and joy in a place deep within if you allow the party inside of you to join the party outside of you. These actions were the beginning of me falling in love with myself in a way that was not harmful, and completely contagious outside my living space. This allowed me to feel joy and to express it everywhere I ventured out. My picnic mindset allowed me to break free of the habitual routine I was living, that had kept me a prisoner most of my life, until I discovered the freedom in this artistic ability to co-create an unstructured routine.

Please do not misunderstand me, I am, like all human life, a creature of habits. I do not leave the house, ever, with dirty dishes in my sink. I do not like to use the dishwasher. It drives me crazy to think about dirty dishes being in limbo, building up enough to fill the machine after waiting two days, because that is how long it takes for our small family to acquire that many dishes to warrant a washing cycle. The thought of those dirty dishes buried behind a nice, enclosed cupboard makes me think about them not being clean. I'm sure some of you are laughing at reading this and some of you are probably shaking your head questioningly. Thinking "You are joking, right?" I hate to say this, but I wish I was. We are all quirky, we all have phobias, and we all have routine. Habits are part of who we are, what we choose. Each one of us can make the effort to stay ahead of all the things that accumulate and build around us, in what we cannot, or will ever be able to control.

I want to share with you one very special picnic I had. It was so precious to me that even today, twenty years later, I can taste it, feel it, smell it, and remember how it taught me this huge lesson of turning action into love.

It was New Year's Eve 2002. That was one of the best and worst times of my spiritual growth. I was gaining new ground, choosing a higher frequency, but the people I had loved for so many years were dropping like flies around me. I understood the choices and the sides people were choosing, it was just difficult trying to keep up with it all. At the time trying to grasp the lessons, and the actions of the lessons, made me hungry and sad at the same time. I was doing my best to survive and to help others through the carnage of the aftermath of the choices. It was incredibly emotional for all involved.

It was the weekend of New Year's Eve. I had decided prior to the weekend that I was going to approach it with a mindful plan that was cemented in happiness. I started to prepare my picnic the whole week before. I carefully planned the menu and sought it out piece by piece. I went the butcher shop and bought a small filet mignon steak. I watched the butcher cut it and wrap it in the special waxed brown paper they use and tie a string around the steak. I paid for it and was grinning the whole time. It was like I had this secret with myself. Each thing I purchased to go with the meal was the same way. The green beans, single baking potato, sour cream, and real butter. I even bought myself a piece of chocolate raspberry cheesecake from a bakery. I did not often drive to London, but I did force myself to do this as it was all part my growth. Although it put me in an uncomfortable state of anxiety, it also forced my hand to grow into a place where I was addressing fear.

I don't know if anyone reading this remembers La Senza, but that is where my heart and soul led me, the weekend before New Years Eve. I purchased quite an expensive pair of lime green, silk pajamas. They were bordered with lime green piping and had two pockets on the front of them. They also had green silk covered buttons and fit me perfectly; they were comfortable and classy. They wrapped up the package, a nice little New Years Eve present just for me. I woke up the next morning, New Years Eve Day, and proceeded to get my picnic ready. I prepared the salad, the wine, meat, and baked potato. I cleaned my small apartment and rented three good chick flicks; one of them was Steel Magnolias. My picnic started to come together as I continued to set the course for the day. I showered and made my hair pretty and then put on the green silk pajamas. I was so happy in my home, in my body, and in my heart space. I purchased a small bottle of champagne, prepared my dinner, and ate it all in my silk pajamas. I watched a movie, drank some wine, and ate my dessert. I watched the rest of the movies in my beautiful silk pajamas. Just before midnight I wrote an intentional list to manifest for my future. I took it out into the winter night and burned it, offering to Source and asking Him to bring full abundance into my new year. These were not resolutions, but manifestations creating new life, dreams, and desires. I applied the brightest lipstick, I could find in my makeup bag, to my lips, lit the last candle of the evening, offered prayers and gratitude. I toasted the New Year and kissed myself goodnight in the mirror, leaving the tattoo of my lips on the glass, and tucked myself into bed. This was my first of many, eventual, personal picnics to come. I have taken time to hone this experience over the years. They are more sporadic now, but every once and a while I get the old tingling, mingling, settling inside; encouraging me to step out of routine and go play with my soul. Picnics for one can be the best kind of picnic you ever experience.

Picnics for one allow you to unravel all the stresses that are made up in moments of living, created within. Stresses to the four chambers of your physical heart, entire soul, complete body, and sharpened mind. Picnics for one can be a secret place you go to. To spend the time, you need to digest the events buried deeply and tucked away many years ago, or could be as recent as a day, or even hour ago. Picnics for one are a necessary timeout. It can teach you new tools you need to grow and is imperative to changing a long-lasting habitual behavior pattern. It can initiate a redirection of the mind or is simply a time to really observe what changes need to happen, and the way you will go about making those changes, to eventually celebrate them.

The possibilities are endless as you take on this new direction, planning, redirecting, following, and then allowing yourself to be fully led into complete action. Over time you will find you are producing actual tangible differences that in turn feed your body natural, long lasting, and sustaining endorphins, by the celebration of you and your journey in the picnic for one mind and soul consciousness.

The Sound of Unhinged Silence

What does it sound like when you make a stand and speak the truth you feel in your heart? When your truth is heard in such way that, when you hear it back for the first time, it sounds like your heart is being pulled out of your chest. Like all the blood is being drained from your body, then your heart is put back into the hole it was pulled out of, and it does not quite fit in the same manner as it did before it was pulled out.

This is painful to write about as it's still a very new scar and the wound is still trying to close around the new space. I understand, as a light worker, we are obligated to live and speak and perform under an unwritten code of unconditional love and ethics. Saying our duty is hard is the understatement of all time. Daily we take on the sore hearts, bruises, and pain of the world that continues to contact us looking for light, hope, answers. We are the ones who choose to work for the source of light, the higher road. There are those who maintain what we believe in, but who can also get caught in the crossfires of opinions and leave us at a crossroads.

This was the case for me last week. I have been doing a live video, on social media, for almost three years now. What started as a fifteen-minute, innocent message, of sharing my voice, and the love light workers attune too, has slowly morphed into a half hour video time that I call "Namaste Thursday". This timeout and check-in with the world have expanded my grown to connection over the years. Some weeks my videos are viewed by a few more than previous weeks, but regardless, it felt good to go out in the world and talk about my own personal experiences and how I have lived through and around them. I have a lovely lady who helps me with the live videos. She believes in the healing and the messages that are shared in the time we are live online. I want to stay focused with the messages, so she and I agree weekly on a topic and then she sets the foundation on the social platform, from where I speak, on the subject matter we have discussed. For me, her professionalism, along with her visual pictures, allows one to read and see what we are discussing prior to the live video. What she does for me is to provide focus and allows me to stay on track and stay on point about the predetermined subject that is pre-posted.

A few days before the last live video I was feeling agitated, edgy even, uncomfortable, and not sleeping well: tossing and turning. I knew deep within me that I was being led to the truth of something that, I had a feeling, may not be overly accepted by the viewers. I had made a personal decision about a choice I felt strongly connected to, respecting myself and my truth enough to voice my thoughts. It was interesting to me, that after the live session I had a few unexpected reactions to my opinion, on this controversial topic. I was literally naive to think I would not be hurt by some people's comments against my personal position, my choice, about this subject. After a full day of sitting with this experience, I asked my friend for her assistance to please take down my video. After another couple of days, I started to thaw out a little, and put my unhinged body slowly back together. I took some time out in silence, trying to give my heart space, and room, to find the beat of normal rhythm again. I decided to take a month off the live videos. Mostly giving myself the time, I needed to find forgiveness in my heart for myself and others who stirred this up. This was a huge learning for me teaching me the bigger meaning of true forgiveness.

Remember when you were young, the times when you had a very bad day at school, or your friends hurt you so badly you could barely breathe? Finding your way home to curl up in a ball and heal. In some ways those timeouts taught me that healing happens, and a good night's sleep can make a very bad situation from the day before, almost a place to find peace in the next day. People, and tempers, cooling down long enough for you to recover and rediscover if there was anything to sort out and mend, or to move on and rebuild. Unfortunately, our society does not allow for a timeout anymore. Our world, the one we are all attached to by social media, does not allow even a recess break. In saying this, I know it was also the direct action I took to posting this on my page in response to some of the comments, both public and personal, to me after the video.

"I just wanted to write a little message, in having some time to digest my last live video. It seems as I marinate in the leftovers of the conversations, exchange of energies. What stayed with me in the aftermath left me feeling the division in our world. This opportunity and the lesson it provided me led me to the experience of what we are living in and what we are living with.

To further this thought and firsthand witness to the exposure of educated council, pain in choices, left me feeling that any human who takes a chance on expressing their personal thoughts leaving themselves vulnerable open to feeling the deep-set pain in our divided world.

This experience gave me a reason and I chose to hold an open heart accompanied by a curiosity of why people think differently.

When there is a connection a bond between people that promotes a positivity, this bond creates energy that sets a spark, inviting compassion, respect, peace, providing a direct visible attainable path to the light.

And when we are disconnecting, the disconnect teaches a lack of compassion, a deep need to be heard, to be justified, this can cause a deep disconnection leading us into darkness and isolation.

I choose to love where someone is at, respecting their choices, holding space for our differences."

How did I feel after this message I posted? I felt flat, sad, unheard, judged, bullied, ridiculed, persecuted, rejected and alone.

I felt and heard the pain, the heartache that the power of my words hurt people I love. I felt betrayed and abandoned. I felt lower than I had in a very long time, as I was sure some of the bonds, I had with others could, and may, forever be broken. Thankfully, I was mistaken. So, what did I choose to do? First, I forgave myself for not being mature, or even prepared, enough to think out what I was trying to voice out. That was my first huge lesson in the recovery of recycling my actions. Stop, pause, reset. I allowed myself to totally forgive the pain I caused others and the pain I caused myself. I forgave all the words exchanged in the heat of the moment, erased them, and offered them up as a gift of love to be erased also from the hearts of others. I tried very hard not to respond out of pain, hurt or anger. Instead, I choose to hold space for all of us wounded in this exchange of thought, choice, and shock, in and through the weaving of this lesson. Will I recover? Yes. Working for Source is a duty, my obligation, and the work that light workers represent.

In my opinion, and I can only speak from my experience and perspective, it's up to me to forgive as quickly as possible, grow a thicker layer of skin, get back on the front line and resume my position of remaining neutral. To forge on and be present for anyone seeking and asking for direction to the light.

I know I won't be the same as I was a week ago, for others who saw me in a different position or a different shade that they were not expecting. I know my only option, to stay on the higher ground, is to forgive things that cause scars and that keep me away from the work we are called to continue. I know that, without my team, I would be nothing less than what we give each other, in the hopes of healing our world and the world around us. I know I have more than enough extra love and prana to share with anyone who is truly seeking whole self, whole truth. I know we all (every single, solitary one of us) deserve this love. I know it starts from within and extends outward to all who take a moment to seek it.

My dying thought, I can only hope will be, is that everyone feels deeply that they are worth love with the understanding it's really who they are.

Marinating In the Slow Stew of Silence

I seem to be using a lot of words these days that take time to discover and uncover the wealth and the gifts buried in their meanings. Sometimes just underneath the surface, or the skin, or even deeper, under layers upon layers of initiation. When I say initiation, it could be like saying a sliver of wood that pierced your skin and got lodged deeply in your flesh. The amount of time it takes before your body can manifest bringing it up to the surface and expelling it. Sometimes, as you know, if it stays under the surface too long the infection, of the invasion of the object, can cause a disturbance or huge discomfort. This is a wake-up call to direct you to act and force the unwanted intruder out. When we take the time to become aware, we need to work together and support each other in the awareness. There always seems to be the right tools to support the effort, combined forces working together to release the pressure and facilitate the exit plan of the intruder.

Let's start with the word "marinate". The most common definition is regarding food, meat specifically. The marinade is used to add moisture or tenderize the meat. There are other meanings of this word. The word marinating, in the online game "Among Us", is a way to hide an imposter among the crewmates in the game. Fellow imposters in the game use the technique as a way of protecting each other or letting crewmates believe that the player is innocent. Imagine my surprise when I read what this word meant, in this sense of the meaning. Suggesting that interacting with people, the people who you call teammates or comrades, in a way that could be deceiving. One other definition is to slowly pickle vegetables, or anything you choose to pickle, over a very slow stewing process. This process takes time, preparation, and marination. Using this method allows the product to age over a longer period, enhancing the results, to become successful in the aging process.

This brings me to talk a bit about why I chose this as the title for this chapter. When reading the description and multiple meanings of this word, it hit me like a hammer on my heart. There have been times when I have deceived myself and my teammates in the interaction of finding my way, discovering my truth, and surviving the harsh reality of the lessons I have had. We all want a connection of love. Someone to align with, support our beliefs, causes and outcomes of our choices. To be on our side, supporting us, agreeing with us, and trusting in our decisions, offering up gifts of loving loyalty. I do not know a person who would not want to live like this as they continue to find their own way in this world. I do know though, after reading what this word also stands for, the side I want to live from.

I prefer to be the softening agent, the ingredient that helps to soften the meat and break down the walls of hardness that make the meat less desirable. I want to be the acting agent that allows the stewing to process. The timing, aging, learning, and supporting the hardness that takes its' own sweet time. Accepting this agent is here to help soften the entire experience. Acceptance in the breaking down, knowing that without the agent, and the ingredients, there would not be a coming together of the two; a softening of the actual physical substance. I know, and choose, to be the ingredient that agrees with taking all the time that is needed. That the time it takes is worth it, waiting for all the ingredients to work together to establish the final product. This stewing, this marinating, allows the slow dance to grow, mature, and become the best outcome for everyone.

Patina is a word I have added to my growing box of power words as well. When you look up this word, it is defined as a green or brown film on the surface of bronze or similar metals, produced by oxidation, over a period of extended time. Oxidation is a chemical reaction of free radicals (oxygen-containing molecules with an uneven number of electrons) with other molecules. Free radicals are used by our bodies to kill invading bacteria. Oxidative stress emerges when a disturbance or an imbalance exists between the free radical formation and the capability of cells to clear and repair them. Factors that may contribute to this are obesity, diets high in fat, sugar and processed foods, smoking, alcohol, pollution, and industrial chemicals. I could go on and on, as the words loop, link, and come full circle as it relates to our bodies of flesh, the combination of living soul energy. I just wanted to reference the powerful word patina, and what that word has come to mean to me. It is a word that I treasure. A word that has earned the color and the texture it represents. To me, patina is a protection that naturally occurs to sustain the life, and the importance of the rich treasure buried very closely, just under its layer. To some, patina is not pretty. In fact, it acts as a camouflage to hide the shiny brilliance underneath, but it's closer than anyone would suspect. Patina is often misunderstood. This protective shield has a job to do is to protect the treasure, the sacred core at all costs. It becomes part of the treasure that is rich and worthy. The treasure that has survived the test of time, long enough to marinate in the slow stewing silence, with a cloak of protection around it.

I often use the words "real estate" when pertaining to the human vessel. It seems to be the biggest war among us, in this world we live in. Taking time to think about what real estate means to me, it means belonging to me; that something of substance belongs to me. My home, material things, and worth. This has made me realize that real estate is what brings many wars about, the need to own, and the power to rule it all.

These words can have more than one meaning, the literal definition, and how they can be relevant in a spiritual sense. In the right context, they can contain a lot of power. How and when these words are used, when aligned in session, contribute to the spiritual gifts they can provide. Becoming more familiar with these words and applying them internally, not just in the external (dictionary) definition of them.

Most of the words I use have historical definitions established or attached to them. Throughout the passing of time, people have mastered these definitions by the actions around the word, making them more powerful. These words can hold their own merit of worth just by their literal definition.

I often choose to use metaphors because they are personal for people. When using a metaphor, combined during a healing experience, the healing settles in and it becomes even more personal. For anyone who does not really know what a metaphor means, a metaphor is a figure of speech that, for the rhetorical effect, directly refers to one thing by mentioning another. A string of connection, connecting the deeper meaning and using it as a guide to relate it personally.

In my personal experience, the human container in which I reside, in conjunction of my soul, needs personal connection for me to learn, feel, hurt, grow, and release. So that I have the experience, along with the equipment to teach, find peace, closure, connection, and global perspectives. Metaphors are descriptive words of action and correlation that allow me to connect the dots. Not only for myself but for others seeking whole self-perspective and personal discovery in the experience.

It Does Not Make It Right; It Just Makes It True

I have not written in this book for well over a month. I had some internal dragons to fight, some growth to experience, and some processing to do, as I continue to release what has been stuck in my internal space. Like saltwater taffy, I have had to pull on it and soften it, so it would be easier to pull out.

I am not going to lie, or even make this chapter into something pretty. The truth is the past six weeks have been diverse, congested, and pain filled. Currently, all over the world, we are collectively going through a huge division, related to a pandemic that we are all trying to find a way to survive in. These changes have brought the best, and the worst, out in all humanity.

During these trying times, separation and segregation can occur because of strong stances, or choices, that differed from others. This behavior may have excluded in-person contact from people with opposing views. This is painful for both parties, the initiator, and the receiver. The initiator, in my case, is the person that is choosing the personal contact. They are sending out a signal that is causing anger, rejection, and judgment. As the receiver in this situation, I am trying to put myself in their position. Initially, my reaction to the initiator, as they did not truly understand my view in this matter, must have hurt them as well. Their message, intended or not, was received by me in a way that caused me to immediately retaliate verbally in response, as a form of defense to my views. Both views are warranted but this was a personal judgment. If our roles were reversed, the initiator would naturally want to take a stand to defend themselves. This could be described as a standoff. It was especially painful, as it caused a divide and a separation, in what is commonly a very like-minded community.

In this situation, everyone has the right to live, or die, by their own personal beliefs and deeply rooted truth. I understand there are two sides of this war of separation, and both sides have ample, educated facts, and documents to back up their views. Each side balancing their own truth with facts for their cause. I truly believe all the fact finding and personal experience with this pandemic are equally yoked, and balanced, for the person who is supporting the side they chose to pick, in their educated findings.

One thing I thought possible is proving not to be true, more and more. It is becoming impossible to stay neutral. To stay in a place of peace and equality, respecting others for their choices, without taking the choices personally. It's becoming more difficult to find peace and comfort for both sides of this controversial subject.

The title I chose for this chapter is that the truth for all, every single one of us, is our birthright to discover for ourselves. It is something we have all lost battles in, relationships in, family, co-workers, and soul workers. Even pieces of our own selves, as we shuffle through the debris of the aftermath of storms, throughout our entire life, living as a human being. We outgrow relationships, or we don't seem to trust in some relationships what we once trusted freely in. In the depths of our own truth, and our own choices, does not always make it right; especially when it leads to destruction of any caliber. Again, I need to make this very clear, this is only my view in my experience of learning the lessons that my life has brought me. By no means do I wish to speak for anyone else, just from my point of view.

During the past six weeks I have experienced some loses, felt broken, sadness in silence, and have been trying to heal from all of it. What has all of this taught me? This has brought me to a place where I can finally say I have discovered that, when I have a personal agenda, I may not consciously even be aware that is has a price tag for me. Most times there is a pain-filled lesson, and a deeper understanding of what truly forgiving another means. I felt something hurled at me during that encounter. I have since chosen to release it, let it go, and have followed up with a spoon full of forgiveness.

Forgiveness is not easy, especially if you once trusted someone, who then uses what you have shared as a weapon to hurl at you, and wounds you. It's almost impossible to not want to defend that kind of attack, and most times all you want to do is hurl something even bigger back. It hurts deeply, to share something with people you thought you could confide in, thought respected you, and understood how sacred the thought was, as sacred as it felt for you when you shared it. When this happens, the falling out shows the truth in the action, does not make it right, it does not, but it does educate you to a place of forgiving the unforgivable. This action allows you to take the deepest dive and let it go without retaliation. This is what I call taking the high road. Releasing the toxins that caused the pain on both sides. Not only for me, but the pain the other person was feeling, to even say or do what it was they did, or how you may have been judged. It's about forgiveness, always. Again, it does not make it right, what you so badly want to defend in your honor, but the forgiving of the action does make it true.

This allows you the freedom to continue to only see the good in the person who felt the need to hurt you, during the interaction between the two of you. Is this even feasible you might ask? Is this even something we can move towards, or raise ourselves enough to (as some people say) the bigger picture?

I will do my best to tell you what works for me in this situation. I first take time to give myself a few minutes timeout after an altercation. Time to react to the shock, pain, judgment, disappointment, and hurt. One might even describe it as stepping out or away from the conflict to a place where I can just sit quietly in silence and sort out the facts amidst the chaos. This did not always come naturally to me. I used to want to stand up and defend myself or reach out to lifelines I knew would listen and take my side, so I could vent and find an ally. I do still have people I talk to about things that bother me, but as most of you will come to understand, you will eventually want to discover, in your growth, to take your own responsibility of being whole, to heart. Most times you are truly on your own to find this clarity in your own journey. I often say we come in alone and naked, and we go home alone and naked. So, finding your own enlightenment can be very rewarding, not to mention you sleep better most nights claiming this responsibility.

When I take the timeout without responding, or slinging any weapons back, I come to see the whole truth. The causes, reactions, and reasons why the offense happened, and the reaction that followed the incident. It is a matter of simple deductions that lead me to the root of the matter. When I see the clarity of the root from all angles, and both perspectives, the clarity is crystal clear. This gives me the truth, even though it may not feel right for me, it gives me the opportunity to forgive first myself in any harm, or hurt I many have caused, or offended in, and then it allows me to forgive the person, or persons who hurt, or judged me. There is a deep feeling of freedom in the forgiveness. The freedom allows healthy new, flourishing, living real estate. For toxic-free energy to take new root, new foundation, internally. This freedom feels like healing clarity that allows you to love deeply. Not just like but love the situation you may have been caught up in or bound too.

I also like to say that there are way more things to discuss in our world than what has kept us captive and a prisoner over the past few years. If we give that energy, and all thoughts to the division happening, we are missing out on all the other things warranted and meaningful to discuss. We, as conscience energy in spirit and body together, are way bigger than this global issue and deserve to

110

spend our precious time exploring other things than our huge differences. It saddens me that we may be missing out in sharing what is left over, to rebuild in a way we can all find peace, equality, and happiness.

Like I have suggested, I have evolved enough to step out of the storm, take a timeout, and admit I know very little about many things. But I continue to open myself up, my most vulnerable self, and explore possibilities daily. Learn new techniques, be open to express, as well as defend, when needed, and try, in the best way possible to find the fine line between selfish and self-absorbed. All I can ever do, to keep myself in this state, is to commit to a form of health, and self-love lessons that serve me for my highest good. This allows me to stay open and aware for anyone who could ever use anything I have learned, and honed, through my own experiences of life, loss, pain, and love. This will always be what I try and offer. Mostly how I make this happen for me, is by accepting myself, forgiving myself, and trying to remain accountable for what I need to forgive within, and what I need to forgive externally.

Intentions Can Be Your New Best Friend

As of late, I have been given the gift of time.   Meaning, I have been able to get away from the old habitual living and lifestyle I have become accustomed to living in, and have established new flow that suits me, as well as preoccupies my time. In other words, I have been able to let go of all things that had kept me bound to routine and allowed myself to freefall into a new place of reality.

Sometimes this kind of change takes a push or a shove into uncomfortable, uncharted territory and can also stir up uncomfortable old scars and dust, buried so deeply that you had forgotten about.   Changing a familiar routine can shift and lift those old fears and triggers to a place of actual uncomfortable feelings, even sadness and grief.

This was my experience recently when I spent a month away from home. I felt a sadness in the silence that I had a very hard time identifying.   I had old memories resurface, ones I thought had long been put to bed, about not so healthy choices, and the losses around them.   I had disturbing moments of moods; the reason, I could not put my finger on.   I came to understand that the routine I was in often camouflaged these hidden, buried pieces, and a bit more closure was required. In my new discomfort I came unhinged, both externally and internally.

What do you do when this happens?   Well, I found a lot of quiet, spiritual places I felt safe in to sit in the silence and allowed the discomfort to rise.   After a while I asked, with intention, what the purpose was, why was it still infecting me, and what did I need to do to release address, and dissect it?   Then asked it to leave my being on all levels.   Taking a stand and talking directly to the incident, personifying it, like it was never invited in the first place, and it was to immediately return to the lower frequency it was born from. It was time to move on and out of me.

This is, by far, easier to type and discuss than to put into action. Some of the hauntings that invaded my soul and mind in this discomfort where extremely hard to identify. It took sitting in the silence, sometimes for a few hours, to dig deep enough to find the other end of the knotted ball of toxins lodged in my solar plexus. Never giving up on a gut feeling and surging deeper than ever. Diving in and finding the other end helped to patiently unravel the root of the issues that were causing the dreams and sleepless nights.

Intentions are a starting point, for someone who really wants to delve into what is literally keeping them from moving into the light and creating internal peace. A place where, if you are willing, will bring you the truest form of peace you could ever hope to experience. A peace that surpasses joy, as you may think you know it. Intentions are the ingredient you must add to every thought, past, present, or even future. If you know the truest form of intent in every single action you have chosen to date, you have the possibility to grow beyond anything you think that will sustain you, into complete wholeness for the rest of your entire life.

Intention, with accountability mixed in, is a sure-fire combination for sustaining this peace through every peak and valley you have yet to experience; releasing all the toxins, pain, and heartaches you have buried, deeper than you even know.

How does intention work? It works by identifying the root of the action you decided on when you intended the action in the first place. This especially works well with past pain, heartache, or loss. Intention helps you identify what you are not willing to let go of and what caused the pain in the first place. Intention works well with ego thought patterns by helping you to justify what you may be having a hard time not being able to forgive, or what warrants you the right to hold on to what you think might be owing you, or who you think owes you an apology for the hurt, indignance, or embarrassment they may have either caused you in their actions. Intentions are entitlement, or justification, when dealing with a past scar tissue or a past grudge.

Intention can be the first step, and the last step, to stop the spread of anything toxic that we grant power to, both internally and externally; by thought, permission, or even our energy to. Intentions are the courage and the truth that can stamp out toxic energy by identifying what the intention reveals. Or even by witnessing the action that allowed you to see the awareness that was concealed in the agenda it was born from. Intentions are powerful, way more powerful than you give them credit for. They could manifest action that, if born from good, creates good. Likewise, if born from misguided greed, fear, or selfishness can cause catastrophic annihilation and a full range of devastating repercussions.

Be aware of your intention. Be specific, check your agenda. Check, and double check, your moral and integral compass. We, as humans, are going to pick some intentions that lead us into a war zone at times. In these lessons, we can only hope we can learn and grow from and come out of the zone with our wholeness still intact. My prayer is that we all learn from this devastation, hurt and self-preservation of survival, as one that leads us to a place of less fear and more community. A conscious consideration of listening and sharing knowledge, agreeing to disagree with enough love to forgive, and the rebuilding of minds and hearts mixed with passion and kindness.

Intentions have become the best part of me. They allow me to remain human, dirty, real, raw, exposed deeply in the trenches, naked, cold, vulnerable, out in the open, feeling like being on a ledge high on a mountain top. In the thick of the sulfur, that seeps from the gutters, allowing me time to wash the dirt off in a clean, clear mountain stream. Intentions are solid; they have a beginning, middle, and end. They form a foundation. It depends on how much time you take to be accountable for your own intention, in thought, deed and then actions. Intentions serve a purpose for how you will roll the dice in your day, how you choose to live in each moment, and provide clarity for your life path. I have decided to become friends with every intentional thought and thought process. Some days I don't succeed. What do I do on those days? I start all over again, after I have digested the outcome and the root cause of why it left me with a stomach-ache or heartache. I take the time to mull it over and retrace my steps until I can identify if the intention was something I instigated, or if I was the victim of an attack from another. By flipping the situation inside out, turning a negative into a positive ending, and wiping the slate clean. How do I do this? I choose to always start with the best ingredient I have ever known; the sure fire one that works like clockwork every time; the glue of everything I ever needed. Forgiveness.

Intention is the magic that manifests when you think bigger than you have ever considered. Intention is proof that what you think, can be turned in to reality. It has the power to change lives, perspective, circumstances, by changing thought into the living reality of action. What does intention mean exactly? To me, an intention is the preface, the commitment to thought spurred on by the power of the action that allows a manifestation. The presence of a thought-out moment in motion.

When you look up the meaning of the word intention or to intend it literally means; what one tends to do or bring about. It could also mean the object for which a prayer, a mass, or a pious act is offered. Intention can also mean a determination to act in a certain way. Intentions, can, and do, have a plural meaning of purpose such as respect, importance, or significance.

When you discover your intentions, the root of what they mean to, and for you, this power can change the impact you have on your leadership. Your words of power are an effective tool to discover your core values and the deep reason of your own personal intentions. This can be very humbling, healing, and educational. As I have suggested in this chapter, intentions can be the bearing of your darkest desires as you manifest what it is your agenda is calling on you into act, or the intentions can soften your thoughts and heart, acting as an agent of higher ground and moral integrity. Both kinds of intentions bring substance and lessons to sort out, discard, or honor.

From my depths, I know which intentions work best for me. The truth that is born from agenda, or intentions. What drives me, and some of the ugliness I had to be accountable for, by recognizing the result of any intended situation? I can continue to choose this higher ground, the path that is significantly different than the easy, well-worn path, forming a new resilience within me, that yes, I have intended. I get to choose that intention, witness it becoming truth, kindness, and ultimate forgiveness. If I decided to intend another selfish inconsiderate example, I experience the result of the inconsideration. I tend to suffer, as we all do, when we choose this intent, the effects of aftershock. I give more consideration, than I ever have before, to what I want my agenda to be and how I intend to teach myself and others by my actions. How to avoid the buried mines of destruction that can, and will, explode. Learning how to dance with my intentions will teach me the best navigational skills I could ever learn externally.

Slow Dance with the Breath of Life

Interesting title for an interesting subject, life. Breath is a sustaining function that allows me to keep on living; something each one of us does several thousand times a day. On average, a person at rest takes about sixteen breaths per minute. This means we breathe about nine hundred and sixty breaths an hour: leading to a staggering twenty-three thousand breaths a day, and about eight million, four hundred thousand breaths a year. Give yourself a moment to take this in and think about how much work it takes your body to cohesively work together. Sustaining this life force to feed, heal, intake oxygen and releasing the carbon waste from within you. This just mystifies me, humbles me, and reminds me just how important breathing is. Something that most of us, myself included, have literally taken for granted.

Several years back, I was lucky enough to have been introduced to meditative prayer meditation. It is driven using a repetitive mantra and requires serious dedication. The format of prayer using a mantra, with the inhale and exhale of breath, repeating the mantra over and over. It was intense, frustrating, and physically exhausting. The teacher reminded me of Yoda on Star Wars, and she meant business. She practiced exactly what she preached and mostly she was a complete state of silence and obedience. It was the first time in my life that I not only had firsthand experience, but that the experience led me to the respect I still hold for the breath of life.

Breathing is a gift. It is a power card all on its' own and has many extraverted means to connect, as a vehicle for flesh and spirit to unite, or reunite through practices, disciplines, intentional prayer, and faith. Your breath can literally become a vehicle of transcending transportation, sometimes to altered states. When you use your breath and either slow it down or speed it up, it can become a partner of connection. I will give you a few examples.

I know in one of my past books I wrote about Sister Jean who was the introduction for me to meditative prayer, but to elaborate a bit more on this experience, she was the introduction for me on what you breathe. What Spirit can do when they work conjunctively with faith, and trust, as one source? As I suggested, I was a newbie, wet-behind-the-ears eager to learn it all in one weekend. I understand now how annoying that must have been, to have such a load of ego clamoring for top marks, in a class you had to take time to learn, and patience to understand. I was trying to catch up and become what I had not yet taken the time to earn. It took me several weekends of dedication in the seminars and repeating the twenty interval sits, several times a day, before I even started to understand the lifetime of silent dedication. Setting my alarm clock an hour early each morning for months and getting out of bed was brutally painful. Honestly, I did it out of obligation to advance, and not because it was fun or enlightening. It took time, and a lot of practice, to finally be prepared enough to be accepted at a seven-day silent retreat in Pennsylvania, PA. I thought at the time I was ready to take on this challenge and become an enlightened soul.

The whole retreat was exhausting, painful, and beyond comprehension in trying to find the words to describe what I felt in the experience. It literally changed the course of how I understood the silence of breath, mixed with dedication and prayer. Simple, structured; so profound. It taught me, like everything good you choose in life, the practice in (and of) it is the teacher that sustains the quality of what it is you are practicing. At the time, I did not realize the potency and practice of this prayer and this breath it did however teach me how to respect the gift I received. I will share more about this with you in the next paragraph, framing the work and the life force of the work force I still connect with every day, in my working world and spiritual practice.

What can I say to bring justice to the breath work I feel so called to share with the world? I can start by saying that the meditational prayer was my introduction to respecting breath in a way I had not ever identified as being powerful. I waited almost a year before I was attuned to my first degree in Reiki and took the time to process my degrees slowly so that I could absorb and work with the newness, the wonder, the tools you receive when attuned.

I was fascinated with the violet breath that I received, along with the Dai Ko Myo Symbol, while being attuned to my 3rd degree of Reiki. I will never forget the feeling of the surge of energy combined with prana life force. The breath was like nothing I had ever experienced, to date. This power stayed with me as in a connection that adhered to my internal soul and attached at the same time to my lungs and breathing. I am trying, the best way I can, to explain the complexity I was trying to understand, as this breathing and combined symbol had no words, but could be felt across the world by people; to all I was sending the symbol and breathe to. I would end sessions with the breath and symbol combined and we could all feel the power of Source in the action and symbol. I would send the breath and symbol out to people in need, pain, fear, and could feel the healing going out in the most beautiful vibrancy. Sent in a cloud of purple, along with the symbol, as I would draw the actual symbol with my breath. To this day, I do this often with clients, one on one, in person, or virtually, or even to people who have no idea they are getting this breath. Administering to these people as a form of intention. When you see someone in need you just do what God calls you to do, spreading his love and the energy of love where it needs to find a place to land.

The act of sending out a violet breath is, first I intend and take in a huge breath of air, as quietly as possible. I close my eyes and see the Dia Ko Myo symbol in my third eye, and release the breath slowly, as the violet joins my breath. I then exhale the remaining air in my lungs and attach it all together, sending it off to the destination, or the person, that it was intended for.

I have been practicing this form of healing and releasing for well over twenty years, and it is like second nature to me now. When the violet breath is calling me to release it, I just don't ever question it. Like a wise woman once told me, violet breath is never, ever wasted. If someone is not in need of it the breath will just softly travel to a person, place, or time that can use it and does need the powerful loving breath to assist them, in the situation they need assistance in.

A few months ago, I was asking Jesus to help me find other ways of healing to offer to people. I have been listening to Jesus for a long time and love when he comes to session and offers up gifts to help others heal. He is always gentle, loving, kind, considerate his presence makes the client seeking healing feel, peace, filled love. Not to mention the amazing heart filter system he has offered up in sessions. I am honored to facilitate and channel on his behalf helping clients receive, this gift has been a beautiful experience. I was asking what else I can do to help people who have deep-seated triggers, and toxins. Pain, so deeply rooted, that it may take an extra tool to help them work this out. Again, I was offered a new breathing technique that truly allows the triggers, and toxins, to be pulled out and released to Source as a means for total cleansing.

I feel so blessed, on so many levels, to have had this intimacy with breath and breathing that is not about me, or ego, or driven by words or thoughts. This powerful breath is Life coming from living, Spirit-filled energy existence that lives in and through God's love. It has no words to adequately identify what it feels like, it

120

must be experienced. It comes from Source and heals without words. It takes huge faith and trust to let go and accept that this form of healing is magical. Miracles happen in the quiet sound of the breath, as it releases what sometimes cannot even be identified.

Faith, blind, unconditional faith, is the key component to experiencing the grace of Spirit. The presence that is not seen with a naked eye, but felt with an open, naked, vulnerable heart. Your soul is willing and able to connect anytime with your ego in an exchange of knowledge that they would be more than happy to share with you, and the breath work that can, and does, heal. Even when you are not present, just intentionally releasing it. In all honesty, it only takes one thought of kindness to spark the engine of releasing healing, in the spiritual world. I have been told many times we are just to be obedient and kind, and to have a loving agenda. Even that is enough to help heal the world way beyond what we need to ever be aware of. So, practice sending loving breaths of life to anyone you think could use it, the gift of your loving gesture. Stand back and be proud of your faith. Hold it like a winning hand at cards, a royal flush that you know you could never lose. Have faith that the one Source who created you, lives within you, loves you beyond adoration, and is with you in every single living, loving breath you take. Be one with this thought and feel the healing that happens for you internally and then surrounds you externally. You are loved, you are worth loving. Your breath of life reminds you more than twenty-three thousand times a day!!

Slow Dancing In the Morning Sun with God

Today started as a normal and ordinary Monday morning, except for the timing of Source, which catapulted the morning into a charcuterie board of spiritual enlightenment. Opening windows, doors, and shutters wide, allowing the beautiful sun kiss from God, landing right smack dab in the middle of my forehead.

My morning started out with a message from someone inviting me to make an appearance on a podcast. This earth angel, Nadia, is talented, humbled, and refined. She is dedicated to someone we both loved in flesh and still feel loved by in Spirit. She has dedicated her love and time by creating "Change Your Thoughts-Change Your Life", found at nadiadelacruze.com. This is a tribute to a man she loved. His mission, his desire to teach all he could, and still does from Spirit. If you're not already a follower, please follow her podcasts, you will not be disappointed. Join her Wayne Dyer Wisdom Community! You will feel connected, supported, overwhelmed by the unconditional love that supports you. It teaches you how to share one spirit, one love, and one way to Source. Through the love this man left behind and supported through dedication, truth, hope, and his passionate quest to teach us this clean way to connection and Source.

This is how my morning started on this simple, pretty, fall day, the morning of October18th, 2021. In the grand scheme of living life large this, for some people, would not even cause a moment to pause in reflection of this opportunity to share faith, talk spiritual shop, by honoring a mentor who never left in spirit, only transitioning from his skin and flesh. For me it is like sitting down with someone at the dinner table and talking about what motivates, inspires, fuels, and teaches us, to forge on as a Shepard for Source. Knowing in faith and trust we are never, ever, on this journey without spiritual guides, teachers, and Source conducting our efforts and aligning our hearts.

As the hour moved on, and Joe and I routinely carried out breakfast, the morning news, and coffee, I received another message from a client who teaches me as much as I have shared with her. She is fabulously aware of God Source, the presence of angels, and all sorts of spiritual connections. She and I have connected in such a powerful way that can only be attributed to Source combination and our intuitive, universal, and often silent, language of the soul.

We inspire each other and have had similar journeys. So, when I receive a message from Violet, every single time it makes me smile first on my face and then resonates in my soul. She had a question about a GoFundMe page this morning that is honoring a great cause. She wanted me to find the link, to authenticate the link for her and a friend, who both wanted to support the cause.

We carried on for a bit in a beautiful exchange of honoring each other, both stating how blessed we are that we were introduced and then she sent me this stunning picture of the morning sun she was given from Source this morning, as a gift. Her words, "This is a good morning. Sunrise about fifteen minutes ago. Have an amazing day." We exchanged a few more words between each other she then says "OMG as I read your text, I felt your energy coming into my soul. It was the coolest feeling sensation ever." She then sends another spectacular picture she took. Her words, "So, I just took a shot of the sun bouncing off the river, look at that energy, it reminds me of how it looks when I see you. Have an amazing day."

I took this message to mean exactly that. I do, honestly, say this to clients, to see beauty in another, in a sunrise, a sunset, a chain of

123

events leading to the reciprocity the joining of hearts and minds cohesively. You must see the beauty by first recognizing the beauty. This allows the mirrored reflection of what you recognize to be beautiful, authentic, and divine, as it brings to life what you see in the loving reflections of the beauty itself. Meaning to see it, you must first be it! So, when Violet sent me the message, the very first thing that I thought about was her depth of understanding beauty and unconditional love. When I told Violet that her morning sharing and offering prompted me to write, and why this chapter "Slow Dancing in the Morning Sun with God" was written. I asked if she wanted to say anything she was feeling, in the moment and that I would put it in this chapter. Her words, "Absolutely, and you won't believe this but, I was thinking of your book when I snapped the photo and sent it to you." Violet goes on further to say, "If we open our eyes and hearts, there is beauty all around us. I guess, it would be in stillness and being alone, this gives us the opportunity to feel the beauty that surrounds us daily." I responded by saying "Slow dancing in the morning sun is like feeling kissed by God."

What does God's kiss feel like? To me it feels like something bigger than I could ever imagine. Like God is calling my name in the breeze on my face, or the gentle pressure of a kiss being planted in the middle of my forehead. The kiss lingers long enough to wake me up and say "Thank you" right out loud! I think any personal relationship starts within and grows to unlimited possibilities that are personal and true to the receiver.

This message, the timing, the perfect silent dance with Source this morning aligned for me the best way to find an ending for this book. It is not something I think about as I write and gather information. Much like the preparation that is happening for me right outside my window, as the squirrels once again start to use this season's temperature to gauge for what is coming in just a few short weeks. We all need to prepare and plan, as we continue to

124

manifest what is yet to be experienced. The third picture, or sign, of validation today for me was when I started up my laptop to write this chapter. The picture was of a beautiful desert sunset casting turquoise velvet blues, and purple hues, mixed with golden oranges, encapsulated by a cactus growing straight up into the sky. Like God handpicked them and spaced them apart so they could spread their arms and reach for Source. I sent this confirmation to Violet, to let her know our theme was carrying on in the most spectacular way, by our Source, our white light loving Father. She responds by saying "Wow that is spectacular. The desert is so amazing."

She is correct the desert teaches strength beyond adversity and even gravity sometimes. The way plants find a way to grow, despite the lack of hydration, they find a way to survive; pushing out life to exist. This reminds me of the true nature of humans searching for whole self. We find a way to dig in, hold tight, let go, heal, release, forgive, and align with our birthright. Our creator who loves us, never leaves us, supports our growth, our lessons, who teaches (above all) to stay humble and kind. Like the desert, we thrive, die, and find new birth. We find a deeper meaning if we dig deep enough to identify the root and set ourselves free from the binds that hold us.

The last thing I would like to leave you with is, we are all worthy of this freedom. We are all capable of rising above the darkness. It lurks in us, its' feeding frenzy designed to contain us in a frozen state of slow growth, so the energy can freeze us, just enough to sustain its' life by draining ours. We are better than this, wiser than this, and worthy of basking in the sun.

Slow Dancing with Spirit has taught me to relax, let go, and be one with Source. Sometimes the dance is a slow rhythm of a waltz, other times the passion of a tango, and often a soft swaying of a gentle box step that repeats and finds comfort in the simple sway of repetition. There are times I can be found singing my lungs out in the shower as I sway back and forth with the shampoo and conditioner bottles. It can be a fun, sassy, unconventional rock song that I find myself moving in time to, with the memories of crazy adolescent days of discovering my body. The memory and reaction to my first kiss, and discovering hidden, treasured passion developing as I continued to find my way in and out of relationships and friendships. Some I am still lucky enough to have.

I will conclude with this thought and prayer for all of you brave enough to take a chance on *Slow Dancing with Silence*. If you decide to internalize, forgive, and eventually clear out the clutter you may find this grand, new internal untampered, untouched space. This space can become your new dance floor, a place to congregate internally for your entirety. A new connection forming a brand-new relationship with you and your spirit. This can change, recharge, and reshape your world. This space may speak to you, your body, your mind, and your soul. This space can advise, teach, and reconnect you to past, releasing and accepting what you want to hang on to for growth and wisdom. The things you choose not to let go may very well teach you the boundaries we are all trying desperately to form. First from within, so we can extend them into the rest of the world, which matters so deeply, to all of us. Silently, this space will teach you all the tools you need to have to go forth and find your way. My promise to you as readers, teachers, seekers of truth and self-love is, that I will daily offer space for you to Source, for the highest good of your highest beings. Live in the luxury of your birthright, something you were born with, something you will transition to, unconditional love. It belongs to you. Claim it, bathe in the glory of the gift of your inheritance. After all, it has always belonged to you.

May love and continued light surround you in all ways, always!
Tracey Pagana

www.ingramcontent.com/pod-product-compliance
Lightning Source LLC
La Vergne TN
LVHW052031080426
835513LV00018B/2269